KT-435-485

COPENHAGEN
ENCOUNTER

CRISTIAN BONETTO
MICHAEL BOOTH

Copenhagen Encounter

Published by Lonely Planet Publications Pty Ltd
ABN 36 005 607 983

Australia	Head Office, Locked Bag 1, Footscray, Vic 3011
	☎ 03 8379 8000 fax 03 8379 8111
	talk2us@lonelyplanet.com.au
USA	150 Linden St, Oakland, CA 94607
	☎ 510 893 8555
	toll free 800 275 8555
	fax 510 893 8572
	info@lonelyplanet.com
UK	Media Centre, 201 Wood Lane, London, W12 7TQ
	☎ 020 8433 1333
	fax 020 8702 0112
	go@lonelyplanet.co.uk

This 2nd edition of *Copenhagen Encounter* was written by Cristian Bonetto. The 1st edition was written by Michael Booth. This title was commissioned in Lonely Planet's London office and produced by: **Commissioning Editors** Jo Potts, Anna Tyler **Coordinating Editor** Susan Paterson **Coordinating Cartographer** Julie Dodkins **Coordinating Layout Designers** Frank Deim, Wibowo Rusli **Assisting Editor** Cathryn Game **Managing Editors** Imogen Bannister, Brigitte Ellemor **Managing Cartographers** Shahara Ahmed, Herman So **Managing Layout Designer** Celia Wood **Cover Research** Jane Hart **Internal Image Research** Aude Vauconsant **Thanks to** Jessica Boland, Carol Jackson, Lisa Knights, Wayne Murphy, Mandy Sierp, Trent Paton

Our Readers Many thanks to the travellers who wrote to us with helpful hints, useful advice and interesting anecdotes. Lars Bolt, Petra Ederer, Frédéric Dobruszkes, Merete Jensen, Richard Lemon and Brad Robertson

All images are copyright of the photographers unless otherwise indicated. Many of the images in this guide are available for licensing from **Lonely Planet Images**: www.lonelyplanetimages.com.

ISBN: 978 1 74179 288 1

10 9 8 7 6 5

Printed in China

HOW TO USE THIS BOOK
Colour-Coding & Maps

Colour-coding is used for symbols on maps and in the text that they relate to (eg all eating venues on the maps and in the text are given a green fork symbol). Each neighbourhood also gets its own colour, and this is used down the edge of the page and throughout that neighbourhood section.

Shaded yellow areas on the maps denote 'areas of interest' – for their historical significance, their attractive architecture or their great bars and restaurants. We encourage you to head to these areas and just start exploring!

Send us your feedback We love to hear from readers – your comments help make our books better. We read every word you send us, and we always guarantee that your feedback goes straight to the appropriate authors. The most useful submissions are rewarded with a free book. To send us your updates and find out about Lonely Planet events, newsletters and travel news visit our award-winning website: *lonelyplanet.com/contact*.

Note: We may edit, reproduce and incorporate your comments in Lonely Planet products such as guidebooks, websites and digital products, so let us know if you don't want your comments reproduced or your name acknowledged. For a copy of our privacy policy visit *lonelyplanet.com/privacy*.

MIX
Paper from
responsible sources

FSC
www.fsc.org   FSC™ C021741

CRISTIAN BONETTO

A weakness for svelte design, adventurous chefs and cycle-toned bodies first drew Cristian Bonetto to Copenhagen. Years later, the Australian-born travel writer and playwright remains gob-smacked at being able to swim in inner-city canals without getting a rash or being labelled clinically insane. He is equally captivated by the city's pro-gressive green policies and high quota of perfect cheekbones. Indeed, Copenhagen's cutting-edge cuisine, fashion and contemporary-art scene con-tinue to inspire this one-time soap scribe, whose musings on travel, trends and popular culture have appeared in Australian, British and Italian publications. When he isn't hunting down the next big thing in the Danish capital, you're likely to find Cristian scouring Sweden, Italy and New York for decent espresso, cheap chic and the perfect shot to post on Facebook. Cristian has contributed to more than 10 Lonely Planet titles to date, including *Sweden, Rome Encounter, Naples & the Amalfi Coast* and *Discover Italy*.

THE PHOTOGRAPHER

Raised in the Scottish Highlands, Jonathan Smith graduated from St Andrews University in 1994 with an MA in German. Unsure of what to do with his life, he took a flight to Vilnius and spent the next four years travelling around the former USSR. Having tried everything from language teaching to translating Lithuanian cookery books into English, Jon resolved to seek his fortune as a freelance travel photographer. Since then Jon's byline has appeared in more than 50 Lonely Planet titles.

Cover photograph Bike riding through Copenhagen, Panoramic Images/Getty Images. **Internal photographs** p24, p28, p30, p105, p115, p153 Christian Alsing/Wonderful Copenhagen (WoCo); p17 Susan Anderson/Getty Images; p151, p157 Morten Bjarnhof/(WoCo); p106 The Coffee Collective; p68 Marco Cristofori/Alamy; p23 Ireneusz Cyranek/(WoCo); p88 Thomas Evaldsen; p48 Rainer Hosch; p97 Ditte Isager; p137 Gunter Lenz/Nordicphotos/Alamy; p14 Niels Poulsen Mus/Alamy; p123 Kenneth Nguyen; p130 Jon Nordstrom/Granola Food Company; p22 SMK Photo; p162 Magnus Ragnvid/(WoCo); p26, p76, p155 Cees Van Roeden/(WoCo); p47 Radisson SAS Royal/(WoCo); p149 The Square/(WoCo); p44 Tivoli/(WoCo); p20 Louise Wilson/Getty Images; p61 Alastair Wiper/Henrik Vibskov; p27, p29, p57, p75, p148 (WoCo). All other photographs by Lonely Planet Images and by Jonathan Smith except p65, p140 Anders Blomqvist; p36 Christer Fredriksson; p70, p83, p85, p136, p150 Martin Llado; p160 Martin Moos.

CONTENTS

Why is our travel information the best in the world? It's simple: our authors are passionate, dedicated travellers. They don't take freebies in exchange for positive coverage so you can be sure the advice you're given is impartial. They travel widely to all the popular spots, and off the beaten track. They don't research using just the internet or phone. They discover new places not included in any other guidebook. They personally visit thousands of hotels, restaurants, palaces, trails, galleries, temples and more. They speak with dozens of locals every day to make sure you get the kind of insider knowledge only a local could tell you. They take pride in getting all the details right, and in telling it how it is. Think you can do it? Find out how at **lonelyplanet.com**.

THIS IS COPENHAGEN

You'd be mistaken in thinking the Danish capital had been designed specifically for the short-break traveller. It's a compact, comprehensive city, but it still manages to cram a millennium of history and culture within its historic heart.

Copenhagen is the most cosmopolitan and accessible of all the Scandinavian capitals. This urban oasis of calm, culture and conviviality is packed with some excellent museums, art galleries and unique monuments, as well as plenty of enchanting, historic streets and other beguiling areas that are perfect for a stroll and a gawp. The same attributes that are said to give its inhabitants one of the highest standards of living in the world – its cleanliness, efficiency, safety and a superb infrastructure – work very much in the visitor's favour as well.

The city is remarkably compact and user-friendly. You can walk across it in a morning, or scoot about on the excellent metro and buses in minutes. Or you can just as easily spend an hour browsing in areas such as Ravnsborggade or Elmegade, or an afternoon getting to know the locals – fluent in English, of course – in a cosy cafe.

Where Copenhagen really excels is in its marriage of old and new. Gabled 17th-century town houses, cobbled squares, canals and green copper spires may define the aesthetic of this royal city but radical architecture, new trends and technology and, of course, that famously discerning design sense are equally in evidence. Copenhagen has largely resisted the tyranny of the chain store so its independent shops – interior design and fashion are major strengths – are a big part of its appeal.

And if you are looking for a fairy-tale experience, nobody does it better than the Danes. Hans Christian Andersen lived in Copenhagen for most of his life, and the architecture and atmosphere that inspired him is waiting to charm, excite and delight you, too.

Top left Cafe culture on Sankt Hans Torv, Nørrebro (p18) **Top right** Antique shopping in Nørrebro (p105) **Bottom** The lion statue at Det Kongelige Bibliotek (p75) looks up at the modern Black Diamond extension, Slotsholmen

Greenland exhibition at the Nationalmuseet (p16)

>1 TIVOLI GARDENS

UNLEASH YOUR INNER CHILD AT TIVOLI GARDENS, DENMARK'S PERENNIALLY POPULAR TOURIST DRAW

Denmark's number 1 tourist destination offers a beguiling blend of flower park, fun park, beer garden and food pavillions located slap-bang in the city centre. It is, in other words, as far removed from Disney as you can get. Depending on your mood, Tivoli will either enchant with its fanciful architecture, theatres and concert halls, boating lakes, world-famous lighting displays, fireworks and – these days – actually quite exciting rides (the Demon rollercoaster is brief but terrifying), or overpower you with its sugary schmaltz. A good tip is to go on Fridays when, during summer, bands play on the open-air stage. You can sometimes catch major international music acts (Sting, Brian Wilson, Tony Bennett) playing for free here; come early to secure a good vantage point.

Every evening, Tivoli wows with a spectacular sound, laser and water show, while its famous fireworks display lights up the sky at the start and end of the summer season, as well as on 15 August (Tivoli's birthday). Scan www.tivoli.dk for times, and also see p44).

>2 RUNDETÅRN

CLIMB THE SPIRE OF THE REMARKABLE RUNDETÅRN FOR A VIEW OVER THE MEDIEVAL HEART OF THE CITY

Haul yourself to the top of the 34.8m-high, red-brick 'Round Tower' and you will be following in the footsteps of such luminaries as King Christian IV, Denmark's famous Renaissance king who built it in 1642, and the hoofsteps of Tsar Peter the Great's horse, all the way up the tower's unique cobbled, spiral ramp to the open-air platform at the top. (Legend has it that someone even drove a car up there in 1902.) From here you'll find the city view has hardly changed since Peter's journey in 1716 and it is the perfect place to get your bearings.

Christian built the Rundetårn, which is attached to Trinitatiskirke (Trinity Church), as an observatory for the famous astronomer Tycho Brahe and it still functions as an excellent stargazing platform (it is the oldest functioning observatory in Europe and is open to the public throughout the year). On the outside wall is a commemorative shield and the letters RFP, which stand for Christian's motto, translated as 'Piety Strengthens the Realm'. Halfway up the tower is an exhibition space with regularly changing displays of art and architecture. See also p55.

>3 CHRISTIANIA

LET YOUR HAIR DOWN IN THE ALTERNATIVE COMMUNITY OF CHRISTIANIA

After 37 years of resistance, Europe's most infamous alternative community finally buckled to mainstream pressure in September 2007, ratifying a treaty that would see Christiania's land ceded to the government for redevelopment over the next ten years. The agreement between Christiania's elders and the government heralded the end to almost four decades of independence from Denmark, the EU and the consumer-driven culture beyond its graffitied walls.

Despite the fact that its counterculture days are numbered, this ramshackle utopian settlement remains one of Copenhagen's most distinctive and memorable experiences. It is home to a diverse bunch of highly principled counterculture pioneers, craftspeople, environmentalists, old-school hippies and, it has to be said, alcoholics and junkies.

Back in 1971, when the community was founded by militant squatters who broke into a group of disused naval barracks in the heart of Christiania, they would probably have been labelled 'drop-outs' or

part of the 'underground'. These days many of their once-radical ideas about recycling, organic food, free love and drug enlightenment have been adopted by the mainstream so, you might wonder, what's the point of Christiania today? Certainly many in Copenhagen have been pushing for its abolition and the developers have been eyeing this piece of land in the well-to-do canal quarter of Christianshavn for years.

While opinions about Christiania's relevance in 21st-century Europe vary, this pot-scented 'Freetown' continues to exude a unique, almost surreal atmosphere – part shambolic circus, part makeshift architectural expo, part urban oasis. Once past the squalid main drag, Pusher St, with its roaming dogs and intimidating drunks, you will find yourself amid crumbling 18th-century barracks and an oddball array of makeshift housing, from converted railway carriages to pyramids, many with attractive waterside views of the old city ramparts. Christiania has several shops, craft studios, cafes and restaurants, including cute-as-a-button vegetarian eatery Morgenstedet (p98). It's also home to legendary live-music venue Loppen (p101). See it while you still can. For more on Christiania and the surrounding area, see p92.

>4 LOUISIANA

TAKE A TRAIN BESIDE THE SEA TO THE MAJESTIC MODERN ART MUSEUM, LOUISIANA

One of the finest collections of international contemporary art in Scandinavia is housed in what is also one of the region's most beautiful museums. Louisiana (named after the founder's wife) is situated beside the waters of the Øresund sea, amid dappled woodland on grassy knolls with views across the water to Sweden. It is an exceptional setting but Louisiana has a collection to match its surroundings (thought not always as tranquil), including a number of pieces from the CoBrA movement (the name stands for 'Copenhagen, Brussels and Amsterdam', the home cities of its members). Notable works are by the leading member, Danish artist Asger Jørn, as well as international names such as Bacon, Warhol, Lichtenstein, Oldenburg, Rauschenburg, Rothko and Picasso. The museum has a very strong sculpture collection – many pieces are on view in the gardens – including works by Miro, Calder, Moore and Max Ernst. There is an entire room dedicated to Giacometti and a number of notable German artworks from the 1970s. Louisiana makes for an excellent afternoon trip; kids, who are well catered for here, love it too. Bring a picnic or enjoy the al fresco food at the museum's own excellent cafe-restaurant with its homemade cakes and Italian sandwiches. A changing program of temporary exhibitions showcasing major artists draws massive crowds. See also p104.

>5 ROSENBORG SLOT

GOGGLE AT THE CROWN JEWELS AND OTHER TREASURES OF ROSENBORG SLOT

One look at the turreted, moated Rosenborg Slot (*slot* can refer to either a castle or a palace) and you might even believe fairy tales can come true. This picturesque early-17th-century castle started out as a royal summer house situated, at that time, well beyond the city walls and grew over the years into this magnificent Renaissance palace. It's now home to part of the stunning royal collection of art, furniture and, in the basement, the crown jewels. Christian IV, Denmark's 'Sun King', began the building's transformation in 1606 and the palace was used as a royal summer residence until Frederik IV built Fredensborg Slot, in mid-Zealand, in the early 18th century. Today the palace's 24 upper rooms, each as it was when their respective kings lived there, contain furnishings and portraits spanning 300 years of the Danish royal family up to the 19th century, but perhaps the main attraction lies in the basement. This is where you will find the crown jewels, including Christian IV's ornate crown, the jewel-studded sword of Christian III and many of the current queen's diamonds and emeralds. The palace overlooks Kongens Have (the King's Garden), an elegant formal park popular with sunbathers and families. For opening hours, see p120.

>6 NATIONALMUSEET

LEARN THE TRUTH ABOUT THE VIKINGS AT NATIONALMUSEET (NATIONAL MUSEUM)

The Danes are fiercely proud of their history and rightly so. There have been times when over half of northern Europe was ruled by Denmark, including most of Scandinavia, Iceland, some of northern Germany and even parts of eastern and southern England. The empire was founded by the Vikings – not nearly as rampaging and brutal as history has made them out to be. That said, they could rape and pillage with the best of them and continued doing so well into the 17th century. This excellent, modern museum covers all of that and more with particularly strong Viking and Renaissance collections, Stone Age finds, rune stones and staggering Bronze Age finds (not least the lurene, or horns, some of which date back more than 3000 years ago and can still produce a note), as well as ancient Egyptian, Roman and Greek artefacts. There is a superb children's museum on the ground floor, packed with castles and costumes, plus a cafe and shop, while the 2nd floor houses a charming toy museum, complete with a veritable village of doll houses. Best of all, entrance is free. See also p42.

>7 SMØRREBRØD

TUCK INTO DENMARK'S MOST FAMOUS EDIBLE OFFERING: THE DANISH OPEN SANDWICH

Sushi and sandwiches have changed the way Danes snack just as they have everywhere else in the Western world, but they still hold a place in their heart for the traditional lunchtime Danish open sandwich, or smørrebrød. There are small takeaway smørrebød restaurants dotted throughout the city each displaying their not always appetising wares in the window (cold boiled eggs with remoulade and beetroot, anyone?).

While tourist brochures often list restaurant Ida Davidsen (on Store Kongensgade, just off Nyhavn) as the doyen of the genre, clued-up locals ditch the camera-toting crowds for Slotskælderen Hos Gitte Kik (p67) and Schønnemann (p66). The latter, a favourite lunch spot of Noma (p99) head chef René Redzepi, peddles more than 90 sandwich toppings, from aquavit-marinated herring to smoked salmon with grated radish, chives and egg yolk. For a more contemporary take on the Danish classic, don't miss Aamanns Takeaway (p121), where combos may include Søvind brie with dried fruit and nut relish.

>8 NØRREBRO

EXPLORE THE COOL SHOPS AND VIBRANT NIGHTLIFE IN NØRREBRO

These days two city quarters vie for the title of hippest place in Copenhagen: Vesterbro (p126) and Nørrebro (p116). Though Vesterbro has its share of great shops and bars – not to mention the ultimate club complex, Vega (p135) – we reckon Nørrebro just shades it in the hip stakes.

Though it isn't very big, you could spend an enjoyable day wandering within the boundaries of this densely packed, ethnically diverse residential, shopping and nightlife area which stretches from the elegant, shallow lakes (built in the 18th century as a fire break) to the north of the city centre. Nørrebro means 'north bridge', after the bridge that spans the lakes and which bears the main shopping street that rumbles through the heart of the district. It passes the historic Assistans Kirkegard (the cemetery that is home to so many Danish artists, writers, thinkers and politicians) and continues to the suburbs beyond. On either side lie fascinating streets such as Blågardsgade, with its street cafes and bars, and Elmegade, crammed with cafes and hipster fashion boutiques. West of Assistens Kirkegård, Jægersborg-gade is a burgeoning strip of small galleries, shops and cafes, including top-notch roaster Coffee Collective (p111). That said, Nørrebro's pulsing heart remains cafe-lined Sankt Hans Torv (Saint Hans Sq), just around the corner from Rust (one of the city's best clubs; see p115) and the excellent independent Empire Cinema complex.

>9 DANISH DESIGN

REDESIGN YOUR LIFE, DANISH STYLE

Is there a more design-conscious nation than Denmark, or a more design-obsessed capital than Copenhagen? Sure, the Italians like a nice sofa and the French have their frocks, but in Denmark design excellence runs deeper than that. The Danes can't lift a fork to their mouth without first determining the designer and scoring the cutlery out of ten for function and form. Visit a Danish home and you will invariably find a Bang & Olufsen stereo in the living room, Poul Henningsen lamps hanging from the ceiling, Arne Jacobsen chairs (or at least copies) in the dining room, and Bodum glassware in the kitchen. This national obsession is celebrated at the Dansk Design Center just across from Tivoli on HC Andersens Boulevard. And to prove the Danes are no chauvinists, the Center usually fills its ground-floor exhibition space with the work of international designers, keeping its Danish classics on permanent display in the basement. See also p42.

>10 THE ROSKILDE & JAZZ FESTIVALS

CELEBRATE THE BEST IN MUSIC, FROM SMOOTH JAZZ TO INDIE POP, AT COPENHAGEN'S HOTTEST FESTIVALS

Thanks to one of those all-too-rare confluences of scheduling for travellers, two of Europe's most celebrated and enjoyable music festivals take place in and close to Copenhagen in early July each year.

The Roskilde Festival is mainland Europe's largest rock festival, drawing crowds of over 70,000. It takes place in fields a 15-minute walk from Roskilde city centre and is renowned for its relaxed, friendly atmosphere. Some of the world's hottest rock and pop acts perform here on several outdoor stages – to give you some idea, the 2010 festival boasted a line-up that included the Prodigy, Alice in Chains and Them Crooked Vultures. That said, the festival is as much about the smaller, more marginal acts as the big names and it is, of course, especially good at identifying new music trends in Scandinavia.

The first festival was held in 1971 and drew a crowd of 10,000. Today over 150 rock, techno, trance, world-music and jazz acts play here;

recent years have even seen some classical performances. You can buy tents on arrival (2295–2795kr in 2011, including festival access) and there is a vast camping place which, as always at this kind of thing, offers the barest of facilities. Come on the Wednesday before the main weekend to nab the best places. For more details, see p26 and p156.

Meanwhile, in Copenhagen the city's Jazz Festival is the biggest entertainment event of the Copenhagen year, with 10 days of music beginning on the first Friday in July. It energises the city like nothing else, not only bringing live music to its streets, canalsides and an eclectic mix of venues, but also creating a tangible buzz of excitement in the air. Usually more than 1000 different concerts are held around the city, in every available space – in fact, the city itself becomes a venue. The first festival took place in 1978. Since that time it has mushroomed into one of Europe's leading jazz events. Over the years, performers have included such renowned names as Dizzy Gillespie, Miles Davis, Sonny Rollins, Oscar Peterson, Ray Charles and Wynton Marsalis. Tony Bennett, Herbie Hancock and Keith Jarrett are regulars, as are Denmark's own Cecilie Norby and David Sanborn. The festival program is usually published in May.

For a selection of the best jazz venues in the city, see p157.

>11 STATENS MUSEUM FOR KUNST

MARVEL AT THE EXCEPTIONAL ART COLLECTION AT STATENS MUSEUM FOR KUNST (NATIONAL GALLERY)

The National Gallery of Denmark is divided into two main sections: the original, late-19th-century building and a spectacular glass-and-concrete extension by architect Anna Mario Indrio. Housed in both are six centuries of art, ranging from medieval works with stylised religious themes through to the Renaissance, and impressive collections of Dutch and Flemish artists including Rubens, Breughel, Rembrandt and Frans Hals. As you would expect, the museum also has the best collection of Danish 19th-century art in the world, featuring leading artists from the Golden Age, such as Eckersberg, Købke, Krøyer, JT Lundbye, Vilhelm Hammershøi, LA Ring and Michael Ancher. Fans of modern art aren't disappointed, either; contemporary Danish artists such as Per Kirkeby, Richard Mortensen and Asger Jørn are on show, as well as foreign stars including Matisse (the museum has 25 of his pieces), Picasso and Braque, and the vibrant new-gen of Danish installation artists. There's a children's section on the ground floor of the new wing, which has plenty of hands-on action on offer. The notable on-site cafe-restaurant means peckish culture-vultures aren't overlooked. See p120.

>COPENHAGEN DIARY

Copenhagen keeps things fairly low key as far as festivals and celebrations go. Aside from the justly famous Copenhagen Jazz Festival and the extravagance of Christmas, the city resists much public hullabaloo. Nevertheless, visitors can still enjoy a packed calendar of events to suit all tastes. The best sources for up-to-date info on events are www.aok.dk and www.visitcopenhagen.com. Another good source of information is the English-language *Copenhagen Post*, available online and from numerous newsagents and kiosks. For art exhibitions, scan www.kopenhagen.dk.

From November to February Copenhageners can practise their figure eights at open-air ice-skating rinks

JANUARY & FEBRUARY

New Year

On the last day of the year many Copenhageners let rip with extravagant, hour-long fireworks displays. These tend to be private events with precious few safety concerns, although there are also some public displays. Thousands congregate in front of the town hall on Rådhuspladsen for the big moment.

Winter Jazz Festival

www.jazz.dk/en/vinter-jazz

From the end of January to early February those suffering from jazz withdrawal after the midyear jazz festival can get their fix from this smaller-scale festival held at various venues through the city.

MARCH & APRIL

Bakken

www.bakken.dk

Denmark's oldest fun park opens on the last weekend in March in the forested deer park of Dyrehaven (p107).

CPH:PIX

www.cphpix.dk

Held over 11 days in April, this is Copenhagen's feature-film festival. Expect more than 160 flicks from Denmark and abroad, as well as a busy program of film-related events, including director and actor Q&As.

A roar of approval for the fun rides at Bakken

Royal guards march to Amalienborg Slot on Dronning Margrethe II's Birthday

Dronning Margrethe II's Birthday

On 16 April the much-loved Danish queen (p80) greets the crowds from the balcony of Amalienborg Slot at noon as soldiers in full ceremonial dress salute her. Thousands flock to pay their respects and even the city buses fly flags in celebration.

Tivoli

www.tivoli.dk

The historic city-centre amusement park (p44) reopens in mid-April for its summer season with a new program of events and concerts, usually including several major international names. The first day is usually packed but the season lasts until the end of the third week in September.

MAY

Labour Day

Workers of the world unite in Fælledparken for union-led picnics, boozing, song and dance. It is not officially a national holiday but is pretty much treated like one!

Ølfestival

www.haandbryg.dk

Specialist beer and microbrewing are booming in Denmark right now. This is the country's largest beer festival, drawing crowds of over 10,000 thirsty attendees.

COPENHAGEN DIARY

Samba rhythms at the Copenhagen Carnival

Brazilian-style shebang with floats, musicians and costumed dancers.

JUNE

Copenhagen Distortion
www.cphdistortion.dk
A five-day celebration of the city's nightlife, held in early June, with the emphasis on clubs and DJ bars.

Skt Hans Aften (St Hans Evening)
The Danes let rip on the longest night of the year with bonfires in parks, gardens and, most popular of all, on the beaches. They burn an effigy of a witch on the pyre (she is said to fly off to the Hartz Mountains in Germany), sing songs and get merry.

Roskilde Festival
www.roskilde-festival.dk
Scandinavia's largest music festival takes place in fields just outside the town of Roskilde, around half an hour by train from Copenhagen. Roskilde draws major international acts and crowds of more than 70,000 music lovers from around the world. See also p156.

Danish Derby
www.galopbane.dk
Denmark's most important horse race is held in late June at the Klampenborg racecourse to the north of the city.

Copenhagen Marathon
www.copenhagenmarathon.dk
Scandinavia's largest marathon is on a Sunday in mid-May and draws around 5000 participants and tens of thousands of spectators.

Copenhagen Carnival
www.copenhagencarnival.dk
Held over three days at Whitsun (50 days after Easter) this is the Danes' take on a

JULY

Copenhagen Jazz Festival

www.jazz.dk

Copenhagen's single largest event, and the largest jazz festival in northern Europe, is held over 10 days in early July. The festival celebrates jazz in all its forms, featuring world-class singers and musicians. This carnival of street performances really brings the city to life; see also p21.

AUGUST

Kulturhavn (Culture Harbour)

www.kulturhavn.dk

This unique event, held during the first week of August, focuses on the harbour and waterways of Copenhagen with a wide program of cultural events, sports and parades, centred on the recently redeveloped 'beach' at Islands Brygge (p100). Most events are free.

Copenhagen Design Week

www.copenhagendesignweek.dk

As befitting one of the great design capitals of the world, Copenhagen has its own biennial design event, with 11 days of design-related seminars, screenings and exhibitions in late August or early September. The event also showcases the work of more than 70 designers competing for the INDEX:award, the world's most lucrative design prize. Upcoming festival years are 2011 and 2013.

Jazz on the water at the Copenhagen Jazz Festival

Glitter, glamour and good times at the Copenhagen Pride parade

Copenhagen Cooking

www.copenhagencooking.dk

Scandinavia's largest food festival focuses on the gourmet end of the food spectrum and is held in venues and restaurants throughout the city – though centred on Øksnehallen – from the end of August to early September.

Copenhagen Pride

www.copenhagenpride.dk

This popular gay and lesbian parade transforms the city centre throughout the day and well into the small hours, with much dancing, flirting and camping. Lots of fun.

SEPTEMBER

Golden Days Festival

www.goldendays.dk

This annual cultural and historic festival runs for three weeks from early September and involves many museums and venues in the city. The theme is different each time – the 2010 festival focused on Denmark in the 18th century, while the 2011 edition plans to explore the theme of Faith.

Buster

www.buster.dk

This thriving children's film festival runs for 11 days in September and features offerings from around the world, plus workshops where children can make their own films.

Art Copenhagen

www.artcph.com

This major art fair showcases the work of more than 500 Nordic artists and attracts more than 9000 visitors.

Copenhagen Blues Festival

www.copenhagenbluesfestival.dk

This international event is held over a week in late September and early October at various venues in the city.

Kopenhagen Contemporary

www.kopenhagencontemporary.dk

This four-day festival celebrates Copenhagen's thriving contemporary-art scene, with both Danish and international talent on display. Events include openings, performances, debates and free guided tours.

OCTOBER

Kulturnatten (Culture Night)

www.kulturnatten.dk

Usually held on the second Friday in October, this wonderful, atmospheric event sees the city's museums, theatres, galleries, libraries and even Rosenborg Slot throw open their doors through the night, with a wide range of special events. Public transport is free this night with the Kulturnatten Pass (85kr).

NOVEMBER

CPH:Dox

www.cphdox.dk

This acclaimed international documentary film festival, now in its ninth year and the largest of its kind in Scandinavia, screens films in several cinemas throughout the city from early to mid-November.

Soaking up the atmosphere of Kulturnatten at Thorvaldsens Museum (p77)

The warm glow of Christmas in Rådhuspladsen (p40)

DECEMBER

Great Christmas Parade

Copenhagen kicks off one of its favourite times of the year with a parade that works its way through the city centre on the first Sunday in December. Father Christmas and his *nisser* (elves) enter the city amid much ballyhoo, ending up in Rådhuspladsen for the lighting of the giant tree.

Tivoli

www.tivoli.dk

Tivoli reopens from mid-November to 23 December for Christmas with a large market and buckets of schmaltz. Attractions include special Christmas tableaux, costumed staff and theatre shows. Fewer rides are operational but the mulled wine and *æbleskiver* (small doughnuts) ought to be ample compensation. See p44.

Christmas

Copenhageners really go to town at this time of year. The shopping streets and shop fronts are extravagantly decorated, Christmas markets pop up around town and there are church concerts galore. From late November, Royal Copenhagen Porcelain (p64) prepares elaborately decorated Christmas tables, with differing themes each year. Danes celebrate Christmas at home on the evening of the 24th with a traditional dinner and dancing round the tree.

Dronning Luises Bridge, Nørrebro

ITINERARIES

ONE DAY

Start at Statens Museum for Kunst (p120), then wander through the serene gardens of Kongens Have (p119) and past Rosenborg Slot (p120) to Kongens Nytorv (p57). Cross the square to Nyhavn for a late-morning beer (p78) then explore the small, boutiquey streets of Store Strand-stræde and Lille Strandstræde behind (p83). After lunch at Schønnemann (p66) head back to Kongens Nytorv and then down Strøget (p57), per-haps stopping to browse in the interior design temple, Illums Bolighus (p62). End up at Rådhuspladsen (p40), from where it's a short walk to Tivoli (p44). Finish the day with a hearty dinner at the Paul (p47).

TWO DAYS

Begin at the Ny Carlsberg Glyptotek (p42) before heading across the road to the Dansk Design Center (p42). On nearby Strædet you will find a marvellous array of smaller, independent antique, fashion and homeware stores (p55). Stop for lunch at Zirup (p69). At Amagertorv, turn right across to Slotsholmen, dominated by Christiansborg Slot (p72), but also home to the Thorvaldsens Museum (p77) and Det Kongelige Bibliotek (p75). Cross the harbour to Christianshavn (p92) and wander beside the canals here. See if you can pick up a ticket for a performance at the Opera House (p100), or spend the evening at Noma restaurant (p99).

THREE DAYS

Explore Istedgade (p129) before heading back to Kødbyen (Meatpack-ing District), with its al fresco cafes and restaurants for lunch. Here you'll also find exhibition space V1 Gallery (p129), or you could relax with one of the many beauty or health treatments at DGI-Byen (p135) just around the corner. Take the S-train from Central Station to Nørreport (p116). Head north and you can explore trendy Nansensgade or head on across the city lakes to Nørrebro (p102) and the shops on Ravnsborggade and Elmegade (p105). Party the night away at Gefärlich (p113) and then Rust (p115) or, from Sundays to Tuesdays, enjoy a quieter dinner at one of the cafes or restaurants nearby (see p108).

Top left Detail of Frederik VII statue and the spire of Børsen (p74) **Top right** Thorvaldsens Museum (p77), Slotsholmen
Bottom Shopping for the latest fashions at Strøget (p56)

Getting to know Copenhagen via the canals of Nyhavn

SUNNY DAY

Start with a swim at the harbour pool at Islands Brygge Havnebadet (p100). Wander the canals of Christianshavn and Christiania (p92), aiming for lunch at Bastionen Og Løven (p98). Take the Harbour Bus (p173) from Knippelsbro to Nyhavn (p78) and walk from there to the Little Mermaid (p82), followed by a tour around the ramparts of Kastellet (p81). From here you can walk virtually across the top of the city centre using only its parks – Østre Anlæg connects to Botanisk Have, from where it is a short hop to Ørsteds Parken (p118). End the day with al fresco sushi at Sticks 'n' Sushi (p122) on nearby Nansensgade.

RAINY DAY

Slotsholmen has Christiansborg Slot (p72), Thorvaldsens Museum (p77), Tøjhusmuseet (p77), Teatermuseet (p77), Kongelige Stalde (p75) and Kongelige Bibliotek (p75), all close together (although you should note

FORWARD PLANNING

In keeping with its generally relaxed, informal vibe, a trip to Copenhagen doesn't require much planning but a little organisation can still help. Buy tickets for the Opera House (p100) and Royal Theatre (p90) well in advance, for instance, and check out www.aok.dk (Alt om København, 'All About Copenhagen') and www.visitcopenhagen.com for news of other upcoming entertainment and events, and for tickets contact www.billetnet.dk or www.billetlugen.dk. If Mette Martinussen's private dinner party restaurant, 1.th (p85) takes your fancy you will need to book three weeks in advance; the same goes for many of the city's Michelin-starred restaurants. For a table at world culinary hot spot Noma (p99), book three months ahead. A week before you leave, check for upcoming art exhibitions at www.kopenhagen.dk and visit www.aok.dk. You can subscribe to the aok.dk newsletter – it's in Danish but you should get the gist. If you'd like to take a walking tour, book at least a week ahead; the same goes for Dine with the Danes (p132). A day before you go, buy and print a ticket for Tivoli at www.shoppen.tivoli.dk (in Danish) to avoid sometimes lengthy queues.

that they are not all open on the same days). You can have lunch in the cafe at the Bibliotek, or at the more expensive Søren K restaurant (p77) looking out at the harbour. From here it's umbrellas ahoy for a quick dash to Nationalmuseet (p42) and, afterwards, a cosy coffee or something stronger in front of the open fire at Nimb Bar (p49). In the evening, the Vega complex (p135) has all your nightlife needs under one roof.

COPENHAGEN ON THE CHEAP

Wednesday is the best day to do things on the cheap. Start at Statens Museum (p120). Pop round the corner to Den Hirschsprungske Samling (free on Wednesdays; p118), and then across Kongens Have to the Davids Samling (always free; p118). Pick up a city bike (p171) and cycle to Christiania (p94) for a curry lunch at Morgenstedet (p98). Every Wednesday in autumn students from the Danish Music Conservatorium stage free classical concerts (see www.onsdagskoncerter.dk), at various venues around the city. Alternatively, every Friday, included in the admission, is a live music performance at Tivoli (p44), often by a major international act. For dinner try retro-fantastic Dyrehaven (p107) in Vesterbro.

>NEIGHBOURHOODS

Summer socialising along the picturesque canal, Nyhavn (p78)

NEIGHBOURHOODS

The great joy of a visit to Copenhagen is that most of the major sights and shops are all within easy reach of each other.

The city's pavements are broad, the cycle paths are religiously respected and it is as flat as a billiard table. Given a relaxed program and a stout pair of shoes, you can easily take in all the city on foot or by bike over three or four days. Alternatively, you can let the excellent bus, harbour bus and metro systems whisk you about the place, and cram even more in.

Copenhagen began on the island of Slotsholmen 1000 years ago and this remains the political heart of Denmark. But today the city centre has expanded to include Rådhuspladsen and Tivoli, where you also find the main concentration of hotels; the pedestrian shopping area, Strøget, and its fascinating side streets; and the royal area north of Nyhavn, stretching to the Little Mermaid, and including the current royal residence, Amalienborg Slot. Look at a map of the city and, broadly, you can see that its heart is contained within the borders formed by HC Andersens Blvd to the west of the city centre, the city lakes to the north, and the harbour, which curves from the east round to the south. Most of the conventional sights – museums, monuments, major shops, sights and restaurants – remain within these areas.

But, of course, museums and posh shops are only part of what Copenhagen has to offer. Beyond the historic centre lie exciting, vital areas that are well worth visiting: the canal quarter, Christianshavn, to the east of the harbour; vibrant Vesterbro and romantic Frederiksberg to the west; the area north of Nørreport Station with its mix of interesting shops, nightlife and sights; and beyond that, to the northwest and northeast, the buzzing nightlife and hip shopping area of Nørrebro, and the embassy quarter, Østerbro.

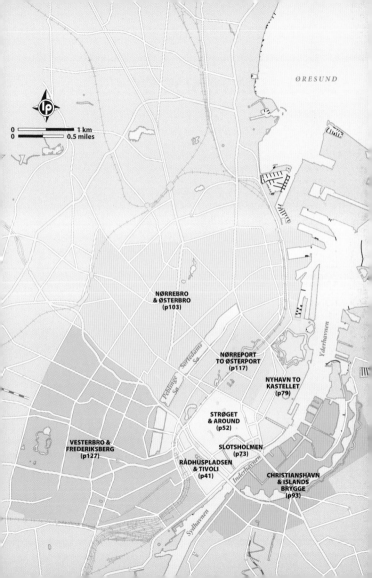

ØRESUND

NØRREBRO
& ØSTERBRO
(p103)

NØRREPORT
TO ØSTERPORT
(p117)

NYHAVN TO
KASTELLET
(p79)

STRØGET
& AROUND
(p52)

VESTERBRO &
FREDERIKSBERG
(p127)

SLOTSHOLMEN
(p73)

RÅDHUSPLADSEN
& TIVOLI
(p41)

CHRISTIANSHAVN
& ISLANDS
BRYGGE
(p93)

0   1 km
0   0.5 miles

>RÅDHUSPLADSEN & TIVOLI

Rådhuspladsen (City Hall Square), Tivoli and Hovedbanegården (Central Station) constitute the heart of downtown Copenhagen. At night Rådhuspladsen is illuminated by neon advertising on the buildings that surround it, leading to – perhaps slightly overstated – comparisons with Times Square. That said, this is the main gathering point for the Danes on important occasions, such as New Year's Eve.

As well as the town hall and the main gate of Tivoli, there are a couple of other landmarks to look out for here. Towering over everything in central Copenhagen is the Radisson SAS Royal Hotel, designed in 1960 by Denmark's master builder, Arne Jacobsen. A short walk away on the northern side of Axeltorv are two distinctive buildings, the multicoloured Palads cinema (p49) and Cirkusbygningen (Circus Building), once a permanent circus venue but which, these days, hosts cheesy 'dinner-and-a-show'-type ventures that are best avoided.

RÅDHUSPLADSEN & TIVOLI

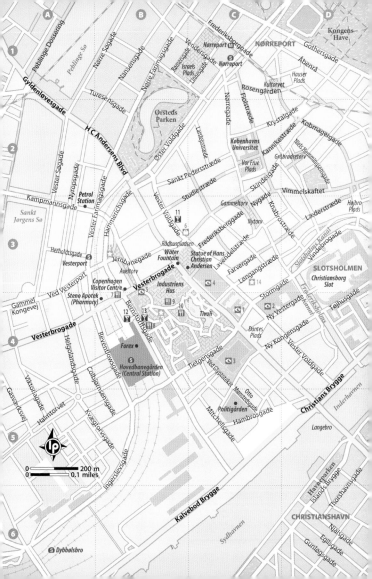

👁 SEE

Danes travel from all over the country to spend the day in Tivoli but Nationalmuseet, Ny Carlsberg Glyptotek and the Dansk Design Center are all major draws here.

📷 DANSK DESIGN CENTER

☎ 33 69 33 69; www.ddc.dk; HC Andersens Blvd 27; adult/concession 50/25kr; 🕙 10am-5pm Mon, Tue, Thu & Fri; 10am-9pm Wed; 11am-4pm Sat & Sun; 🚇 Central Station 🚌 33; ♿
Denmark's design museum offers both an imaginative changing exhibition space on the ground floor and a permanent collection of Danish design classics in the

time for each other kr. 30,–
Pills and thrills at the Dansk Design Center

---

basement. There's a good cafe and gift shop too.

📷 NATIONALMUSEET

☎ 33 13 44 11; www.natmus.dk; Ny Vestergade 10; admission free; 🕙 10am-5pm Tue-Sun; 🚌 1A, 2A, 6A, 11, 12, 15; ♿
Denmark's superb national history museum. See also p16.

📷 NY CARLSBERG GLYPTOTEK

☎ 33 41 81 41; www.glyptoteket.dk; Dantes Plads 7; adult/child 60kr/free, Sun free; 🕙 11am-5pm Tue-Sun; 🚇 Central Station 🚌 1A, 2A, 11, 33; ♿
This exceptional collection of paintings and sculptures, founded by beer baron Carl Jacobsen in 1888, has recently been extensively renovated. The Winter Garden (with a lovely, homely cafe) that lies at the heart of this vaguely Venetian-looking building has now been returned to its former glory and from here you can meander through a magnificent post-impressionist collection, including a large number

of works by Gauguin and pieces by Cézanne, Van Gogh, Monet and Degas, as well as viewing 5000 years' worth of sculpture.

RÅDHUSET (TOWN HALL)

☎ 33 66 25 82; www.kk.dk; guided tour Rådhus/ Verdensur/ tower 30/10/20kr; 🕑 8.30am-4.30pm Mon-Fri & 10am-1pm Sat, town hall guided tour 3pm Mon-Fri & 10am Sat, tower guided tour 11am & 2pm Mon-Fri & noon Sat; 🚇 Central Station 🚌 2A, 5A, 6A, 10, 12, 14, 26, 29, 33, 67, 68, 69; ♿

This sturdy, national romantic-style town hall is the centre of political power in the city. On the right as you enter is a unique

LIKING THE VIKINGS

The Viking empire replaced the Romans as the pre-eminent force in northern Europe for 300 years from the late 8th century. In their state-of-the-art longships, this race of Norsemen – made up of Norwegians, Swedes, Icelanders and Danes – traded and raided as far north as Scotland, west to Ireland and modern-day Canada, east to the Volga River and as far south as North Africa. They colonised much of Ireland and England. The Viking era ended with the arrival of Christianity in the north, around 1066.

The Vikings are famous for their rune stones and horned helmets – the latter in fact misattributed to them (horned helmets were a Bronze Age fashion). They also gave us Bluetooth, or at least the name, which comes from one of their kings, Harold Bluetooth (it's a Danish invention, by the way). If you ask them, the Danes are proud of their Viking ancestors but they tend to keep it low-key. One of the few places you can learn more about them in Copenhagen is Nationalmuseet (left) but if you want to see their extraordinary sailing vessels for yourself, we recommend a trip to Roskilde's **Viking Ship Museum** (☎ 46 30 03 00; www. vikingeskibsmuseet.dk; Vindeboder 12; May-Sep adult/child under 18yr 100kr/free, Oct-Apr 70kr/free; 🕑 10am-5pm; 🚇 Roskilde, 🚌 603), 25 minutes west of Copenhagen by train.

Towards the end of the Viking era, the narrow end of the Roskilde fjord was deliberately blocked by the locals, who sailed five ships out onto the water and scuttled them with several tons of stones. Latter-day locals had long harboured a hunch that there was something out there, but it wasn't until researchers made a series of dives in the late 1950s that the truth was revealed, and excavations began in 1962 to raise the ancient vessels. The fragments found were reassembled and put on display in a purpose-built museum, overlooking the water, which opened in 1969. In the 1990s nine more ships were discovered during construction work – some from the Middle Ages, but yet more from the Viking era including one 36m in length. Today the harbour here is an excellent day trip, with open-air workshops, a restaurant and, in the summer, trips on the fjord in recreations of Viking ships or on **MS Sagafjord** (☎ 46 75 64 60; www.sagafjord.dk).

clock, the Verdensur, designed by the Danish astromechanic Jens Olsen and built in 1955 at a cost of 1,000,000kr. It displays not only the time locally but also things like the solar time, sunrises and sunsets and even the Gregorian calendar. You can also climb the town hall tower for a great view of the city. Minimum of four people per tour.

☉ TIVOLI

☎ 33 15 10 01; www.tivoli.dk; Vesterbro-gade 3; adult/child under 8yr 95kr/free, multiride ticket adult/child 205/170kr; ☼ 11am-11pm Sun-Thu, to midnight Fri & Sat mid-Apr–end Sep, 10am-10pm daily mid-end Oct, 11am-10pm or 11pm

mid-Nov-Dec; 🚇 Central Station 🚍 5A, 6A, 11, 26, 30, 40, 47, 250S; ♿
There are three entrances to Tivoli: the main one on Vesterbro-gade, another opposite the main entrance to the Central Station and one on HC Andersens Blvd opposite Ny Carlsberg Glyptotek. You pay both for entrance and then again for whatever rides you choose thereafter (usually around 25kr each), although a multiride ticket covers all the rides, among them the Star Flyer, reputedly the world's tallest carousel. There are also plenty of free shows, including the Saturday-night fireworks (on show from mid-June to mid-August), the nightly

The spectacle of Tivoli at night

laser show spectacular and the live band at Plænen (p49) every Friday at 10pm from mid-April to late September. At the time of research, opening times and prices for 2011 had not been confirmed and may therefore vary. Check the website for updates, and also see p10 for more information.

THE FAIRY TALE OF HIS LIFE

For the Danes, Hans Christian Andersen is Shakespeare, Goethe and Dickens rolled into one. That may sound a little excessive for a fairy-tale writer, but Andersen was far more than that. As well as single-handedly revolutionising children's literature (*Alice in Wonderland*, the works of Roald Dahl and even Harry Potter owe him a debt), he wrote novels, plays and several fascinating travel books.

Stories such as *The Little Mermaid*, *The Emperor's New Clothes* and *The Ugly Duckling* have been translated into over 170 languages and are embedded in the global literary consciousness like few others. Even today, over centuries since his birth, their themes are as relevant and universal as ever.

Andersen was born in Odense on 2 April 1805. In three autobiographies – including *The Fairy Tale of My Life* – he mythologised his childhood as poor but idyllic. But the truth was his mother (a washerwoman) and his father (a cobbler) were not married when he was conceived, and his father died when Andersen was 11.

Andersen left for Copenhagen soon after, an uneducated, gauche 14-year-old on a classic fairy-tale mission: to make his fortune in the big city. He tried and failed at various occupations until he eventually found international success with his writing, initially his poems and plays, and then his first volume of short stories.

Andersen lived the rest of his life in the city at various addresses, primarily on **Nyhavn** (p90) but also in the **Hotel d'Angleterre** (p148) and, in his youth, in the attic of what is now **Magasin du Nord** (p63). You can visit the rooms in the department store; they remain preserved much as they would have been when he lived there.

His later success and accompanying wealth were some compensation for what was an otherwise deeply troubled life. Andersen was a neurotic, sexually ambivalent, highly strung hypochondriac – he left a card reading 'I am only apparently dead' beside his bed each night because of a morbid fear of falling into a deep sleep, being taken for dead and buried alive.

It all perhaps goes some way to explaining why he was such a restless nomad to the last. He travelled further than any of his compatriots, most notably in 1840–41 when he journeyed as far as Istanbul and wrote of his experiences in the highly accomplished travelogue *A Poet's Bazaar*.

Andersen died of liver cancer, at the grand old age of 70, in 1875. He is buried in **Assistens Kirkegård** (p104).

NEIGHBOURHOODS

RÅDHUSPLADSEN & TIVOLI

🛍 SHOP

Rådhuspladsen is not a major shopping destination. There is a small arcade to the left of the main entrance to Tivoli on Vesterbrogade, which has an Irma supermarket and a bakery, HC Andersen Bageri, where you can stock up for a picnic in Tivoli.

📕 POLITIKENS BOGHALLEN
Books
☎ 33 47 25 60; Rådhuspladsen 37;
🕑 10am-7pm Mon-Fri, to 4pm Sat;
🚍 10, 12, 14, 26, 29

This is the city's biggest book store, with a large English-language section.

🍴 EAT

The area around Rådhuspladsen has its fair share of fast food outlets, but there are several more appealing alternatives on offer.

🍴 ALBERTO K *Italian*　€€€
☎ 33 42 61 61; www.alberto-k.dk;
Radisson SAS Royal Hotel, Level 20, Hammerischegade 1; 🕑 6-9.45pm Mon-Sat;
🚇 S-train Vesterport, Central Station
🚍 5A, 6A, 26, 30, 40, 47; ♿

The modern Italian cuisine served here is a match for the panoramic view at this 20th-floor hotel restaurant, which is really saying something. The menu blends locally sourced game and fish with

Eating out at Rådhuspladsen

Italian ingredients – the venison with aged balsamic, pimento and a roast garlic and potato terrine being a good example. The restaurant has a well-established, international wine cellar.

🍴 ANDERSEN BAKERY HOT DOG KIOSK *Bakery*   €
☎ 33 75 07 35; Bernstorffsgade 5; 🕙 11am-7pm; 🚇 Central Station 🚌 11, 15, 30, 40, 66, 250S

Made with organic pork sausage, Bornholm mustard and a chanterelle sauce, Andersen's Grand Danois hot dog (50kr) is quite possibly Denmark's best. The kiosk is just to the left of Andersen's main entrance.

🍴 GRØFTEN *Danish*   €€
☎ 33 75 06 75; Tivoli; 🕙 noon-10pm Tue-Sun; 🚇 Central Station 🚌 5A, 6A, 11, 26, 30, 40; 👍

One of Tivoli's more traditional Danish offerings, housed in its oldest building and with a menu that includes several different smørrebrød (p17).

🍴 PAUL
Modern European   €€€
☎ 33 75 07 75; www.thepaul.dk; Tivoli; 🕙 lunch & dinner Apr-Sep; 🚇 Central Station 🚌 5A, 6A, 11, 26, 30, 40; 👍

Located in a crescent conservatory designed by Poul Henningsen, this Michelin-starred restaurant – named after its English owner,

Every seat is a window seat at Alberto K

Paul Cunningham – is one of the city's finest, serving elegant and refined modern European food.

🍸 DRINK

The bars and pubs opposite Tivoli and on Strøget are a popular Saturday night destination for a young, boozy crowd but there are a few other, more interesting places close by.

🍸 BJØRGS *Cafe-Bar*
☎ 33 14 53 20; www.cafebjorgs.dk; Vester Voldgade 19; 🕙 9am-midnight Mon & Tue, 9am-1am Wed & Thu, 9am-2am Fri, 10am-2am Sat, 10am-midnight Sun; 🚌 10, 12, 14, 26, 29

Jens Martin Skibsted
Designer and cofounder of Biomega, Danish bicycle company

Danes love cycling because… Of the flat terrain, their regard for social experimentation and the absence of a local car industry. Plus the cool factor. **A perfect cycling route…** Start at Tivoli (p44), pass Ny Carlsberg Glyptoteket (p42) and Børsen (p74), ride along Christianshavn canal, through Christiania (p94) and to the new Opera House (p100). Take the harbour bus (a boat) to Nyhavn for a beer, ride to the Little Mermaid (p82) and to Statens Museum for Kunst (p120) via Kastellet. Head to Rosenborg Slot (p120) and chill in Kongens Have (p118). **Cycling etiquette includes…** Looking back before overtaking, raising your hand before stopping and extending your arm when turning. **By 2020…** People will express themselves through their bikes, with two-wheel equivalents of Ferraris, Fords and Fiats. By 2050 bikes will be smart, electric and part of the grid.

This L-shaped cafe-bar is a good people-watching venue and is a popular after-work drinks haunt. It also serves simple burgers and salads.

▼ LIBRARY BAR *Bar*
☎ 33 14 92 62; www.profilhotels.com; Copenhagen Plaza; Bernstorffsgade 4; 🕑 4-11pm Mon-Thu, to 1am Fri & Sat; 🚇 Central Station 🚌 10, 11, 15, 26, 30, 40, 47; ♿

The Plaza Hotel's small bar mimics a classic London gentlemen's club, with leather chairs, an open fire and shelves lined with books.

▼ NIMB BAR *Cocktail Bar*
☎ 88 70 00 00; www.nimb.dk; Bernstorffsgade 5; 🕑 6pm-midnight Sun-Wed, to 1am Thu-Sat; 🚇 Central Station 🚌 11, 15, 30, 40, 66, 250S

If you fancy chandeliers, contemporary murals and an open fire with your libations, make sure this ballroom bar is on your list. Kick-started by legendary bartender Angus Winchester, Nimb's cocktails are seasonal, classically styled and wittily named (we dare you to order the Pornstar Martini).

★ PLAY
This is the heart of the city's big-screen and multiplex cinema district but Tivoli and other smaller-scale venues offer some variety.

■ MOJO *Live Music*
☎ 33 11 64 53; www.mojo.dk in Danish; Løngangstræde 21; admission free-150kr; 🕑 8pm-5am; 🚇 Central Station 🚌 6A, 11, 12, 33

Mojo is one of the city's leading blues venues, hosting live entertainment every night of the week.

■ PALADS CINEMA *Cinema*
☎ 70 13 12 11; www.kino.dk; Axeltorv 9; 🚇 S-train Vesterport, Central Station 🚌 5A, 30, 11, 14, 15; ♿

A multiplex, yes, but one with a garish charm. Palads Cinema offers a large number of choices in both Danish and international films (subtitled in Danish).

■ TIVOLI'S KONCERTSAL & PLÆNEN *Live Music*
☎ 33 15 10 12; www.tivoli.dk; Tivoli, Vesterbrogade 3; 🚇 Central Station 🚌 5A, 6A, 26, 11, 30, 40; ♿

Copenhagen's largest concert hall attracts major international acts, often of the easy listening/musical theatre variety – Elvis Costello played here in 2010. Improbably, this historic building is now also home to Europe's longest saltwater aquarium. Meanwhile, every Friday at 10pm you'll find a major Danish or international pop act performing for free at the open-air stage, Plænen.

>STRØGET & AROUND

Strøget is Copenhagen's main pedestrian shopping street (it's actually made up of several streets and squares), said to be the longest of its kind in Europe, and a major gathering point for locals. This is the living heart of the city, made up of a maze of well-preserved, 18th- and 19th-century streets lined with pretty town houses, copper-spired churches and cobbled squares, and usually thronging with a hectic blend of shoppers and cyclists. Cars struggle here as most of the streets around Strøget are either pedestrian or unfathomable one-ways, so it's best to explore the fantastic range of small, independent shops, cosy cafes and stylish restaurants on foot.

STRØGET & AROUND

Please see over for map

👁 SEE

🔲 CARITAS SPRINGVANDET

Gammeltorv

The Charity Fountain is the most beautiful in Copenhagen. It was built in 1608 and is a popular rallying point for buskers.

🔲 DOMHUSET

Nytorv; 🕙 **8.30am-3pm Mon-Fri;**
🚌 **6A;** ♿

Copenhagen's pink-stucco, neoclassical court house was designed by CF Hansen (also responsible for Vor Frue Kirke, p56) and built in 1815. It is linked by its own 'bridge of sighs' to cells across the road on Slutterigade. The words inscribed above the courthouse steps, 'Med Lov Skal Man Land Bygge' (With Law Shall One Build the Land), are taken from the Jutland Code that codified laws in Denmark in 1241. You can take a peek inside, although they don't encourage casual visitors.

🔲 GAMMEL STRAND

🚌 **6A;** ♿

Gammel Strand (Old Beach) fronts the canal that partially encircles the island of Slotsholmen. This

Nineteenth-century houses line the canals of Gammel Strand

perfectly preserved row of 18th- and 19th-century town houses, with its restaurants and cafes, is among the most picturesque in Copenhagen and a great place for an outdoor drink on a sunny day. This used to be the site of the old fish market, a fact that is commemorated by the statue of the fishwife beside Højbro. On the other side of the bridge, in the waters of the canal itself, you can see a statue of a merman and his children, while facing the fishwife is a grander statue of Bishop Absalon, who founded Copenhagen over 1000 years ago. You can also catch the canal tour boats from here (see p177).

🅒 HELLIGÅNDSKIRKEN
☎ 33 15 41 44; Nils Hemmingsensgade 5, Strøget; 🕑 noon-4pm Mon-Fri & services on Sun; 🚌 6A; ♿
The Church of the Holy Spirit, located opposite clothing store H&M, dates from the 15th century and sits on the site of an even older monastery founded in the 13th century. It often hosts secondhand book sales.

🅒 KUNSTFORENINGEN GL STRAND
☎ 33 36 02 60; www.glstrand.dk; Gammel Strand 48; adult/under 17yr/concession 55/free/40kr; 🕑 11am-5pm Tue & Fri-Sun, to 8pm Wed & Thu; 🚌 6A

Back from a major revamp, the HQ of Denmark's artists' union continues to present local and international artistic talent. A recent exhibition showcased the creative output of cult American film director David Lynch.

🅒 KUNSTHALLEN NIKOLAJ
☎ 33 18 17 80; www.kunsthallen nikolaj.dk; Nikolaj Plads 10; adult/ concession 20kr/free, Wed free; 🕑 noon-5pm Tue, Wed & Fri-Sun, to 9pm Thu; Ⓜ Kongens Nytorv 🚌 11, 350S; ♿
This 13th-century church is now the home of the Copenhagen Contemporary Arts Centre, which hosts around half a dozen exhibitions of contemporary art each year.

🅒 LATIN QUARTER
🚌 6A; ♿
This small corner of the city centre has little in common with the Latin Quarter of Paris, but gets its nickname from the presence of the university (now home to the law faculty) and the secondhand bookshops and cafes that grew up around it. The Latin Quarter stretches east from Vor Frue Plads along Store Kannikestræde and Skindergade to Købmagergade, via the pretty Gråbrødretorv (Grey Friars' Sq, founded in the mid-17th century), with its open-air restaurants and

CHEER UP, IT'S NOT ALL BAD…

Denmark's most famous philosopher, Søren Kierkegaard, was regarded as 'the father of existentialism'. Born into a prosperous Copenhagen family on 5 May 1813 (in a house on Nytorv where the Danske Bank now stands), he inherited a large fortune and used it to finance his musings on morality and God. Kierkegaard studied theology and philosophy at Copenhagen University but it was being rejected by his one great love, Regine Olsen, that proved to be the major impetus behind his writing. His first great work, *Either/Or* (1843) examined the conflict between aesthetic pleasures and the ethical life, followed by *Fear and Trembling* and the less catchy *Concluding Unscientific Postscript to the Philosophical Fragments*. One of his earliest works was a complex criticism of his Copenhagen contemporary Hans Christian Andersen. Andersen would be just one of many enemies the cantankerous Kierkegaard would make in a short life that ended in death from exhaustion in 1855.

bars, and north up Fiolstræde to Nørre Voldgade. There are several inviting cafes, bars and interesting shops here.

◉ PISSERENDEN
🚌 6A, 12, 26, 29, 33

This cosy grid of shopping streets lies immediately to the north of Strøget. Its shops are younger and more 'alternative' than the main drag, with clothing stores, secondhand CD shops, cafes, bars and bagel shops. A century or so ago this was a rather unsavoury part of town, full of brothels and *bodegas* (pubs), but these days it is a bustling network of streets (Studiestræde, Larsbjørnstræde and Vestergade are the main ones), popular with students and creative types from the advertising and design studios nearby.

◉ RUNDETÅRN
☎ 33 73 03 73; www.rundetaarn.dk; Købmagergade 52A; adult/child 25/5kr; ☀ tower & observatory 10am-8pm end May-end Sep, to 5pm rest of yr, 7-10pm Tue & Wed mid-Oct–mid-Mar; Ⓜ Nørreport Ⓡ S-train Nørreport 🚌 350S

One of the city's most striking landmarks (see also p11).

◉ STRÆDET
🚌 6A; ♿

Running parallel to Strøget to the south is Strædet, perhaps the most beautiful shopping street in the city. It is less grand than Strøget, but Strædet's two streets, Kompagnistræde and Læderstræde, are far more charming and packed with less-mainstream shops. Its strong points are its excellent range of independent jewellers and antique silver shops, but there are several good cafes here, too.

Shopaholics of the world unite at Strøget

Though supposedly pedestrian, cars and, more perilously, fast-moving cyclists do still venture this way, so keep your wits about you.

◉ VOR FRUE KIRKE

☎ 33 37 65 40; www.koebenhavnsdom kirke.dk; Nørregade 8; admission free; ◷ 8am-5pm; ⊛ S-train Nørreport ⊟ 6A; ♿

Copenhagen's Domkirke (cathedral) is an austere, neoclassical building designed by CF Hansen and dates back to 1829. Crown Prince Frederik married Mary Donaldson here in 2004 amid great celebration. It is worth visiting to see the imposing sculptures of Christ and the 12 apostles by Denmark's great neoclassical sculptor, Bertel Thorvaldsen (see p77).

▢ SHOP

Running through the heart of what must be one of the most charming city centres in Northern Europe are the pedestrian streets that together make up Strøget (pronounced 'stroll'). Strøget begins at Rådhuspladsen with some downmarket clothing stores, pubs and fast-food joints, but picks up the pace when it arrives at the picturesque double squares of Nytorv and Gammeltorv (Old and New Square). From here the shops move progressively upmarket – although remaining resolutely mainstream – past the Royal Copenhagen stores on Amagertorv, with its famous 'stork fountain', and onwards to Strøget's conclusion at Kongens Nytorv.

We can't help feeling Strøget is starting to lose its way as a must-see shopping destination.

International chains are encroaching and the western end is a not-terribly-appealing mix of kebab kiosks and budget clothing chains, while to the east are the kind of high-end labels – Hermes, Gucci, Louis Vuitton – you can find in any big city in Europe.

However – and it's a big however – if you take a detour off the main drag, down the side streets, you'll find some real retail treasures. On Strædet (p55), in Pisserenden (p55) and within the area bordered by Strøget, Købmagergade, Kronprinsensgade and Gothersgade, there are dozens of small (and some large) independent shops,

The interior of the neoclassical Vor Frue Kirke lights up at Christmas time

selling locally designed homewares, jewellery, clothing, ceramics and glassware. The latter area is the centre of Copenhagen's high-end, establishment fashion scene, home to several flagship stores of notable Scandinavian designers, such as Bruuns Bazaar (p59) and Day Birger Mikkelsen (p59). It's here that you'll find the city's so-called 'fashion street', Kronprinsensgade, although we would argue that places such as Elmegade and Ravnsborggade in Nørrebro are usurping it these days.

Please note that in cases of shops on or close to Strøget, the bus numbers given are those that go closest to the shops in question, but there may still be some walking to do.

BIRGER CHRISTENSEN
Fashion

☎ 33 11 55 55; www.birger-christensen.com; Østergade 38, Strøget; ⏰ 10am-6pm Mon-Thu, to 7pm Fri, to 4pm Sat; Ⓜ Kongens Nytorv ☒ 15, 19, 26, 1A

The city's pre-eminent upmarket clothing store sells a wide range of Danish and international brands for both men and women, including Prada, Chanel and YSL. Known in Denmark for its furs.

Hunting for the latest fashion and design on the streets of Strøget

BRUUNS BAZAAR *Fashion*
☎ 33 32 19 99; www.bruunsbazaar.com; Kronprinsensgade 8 & 9; ⏱ 10am-6pm Mon-Thu, to 7pm Fri, to 4pm Sat; 🚌 350S

Bruuns Bazaar is now an internationally recognised fashion label selling archetypal, contemporary Scandinavian style around the world. This is where the men's and women's Bruuns Bazaar stores began – they also stock other well-known brands.

CASA SHOP
Homewares/Furniture
☎ 33 32 70 41; www.casagroup.com; Store Regnegade 2; ⏱ 10am-5.30pm Mon-Thu, to 6pm Fri, to 3pm Sat; 🚌 350S

One of the major – and most expensive – furniture and homewares stores in the city, packed full of modern, international (well, mostly Italian) brands beloved of the childless and well-heeled.

DAY BIRGER MIKKELSEN
Fashion
☎ 33 45 88 80; www.day.dk; Pilestræde 16; ⏱ 10am-6pm Mon-Thu, to 7pm Fri, to 5pm Sat; 🚌 350S; ♿

The magnificent new flagship store for this leading Danish brand is right in the heart of the mainstream fashion district. Birger's clothes are elegant, classic and sexy, with just a hint of hippy (and that's just the menswear). Designer Malene Birger's own shop (she is no longer part of the Day group) is just around the corner on Antonigade 10 and has the same opening hours.

FILIPPA K *Fashion*
☎ 33 93 80 00; www.filippa-k.com; Ny Østergade 13; ⏱ 11am-6pm Mon-Thu, to 7pm Fri, to 4pm Sat; 🚌 350S

This is Swedish designer Filippa Kihlborg's flagship Danish store, selling her simple, modern, often monochromatic men's and women's ranges – both day-to-day stuff and more dressy partywear.

FRYDENDAHL
Homewares/Gifts
☎ 33 13 63 01; www.janfrydendahl.dk; Store Regnegade 1; ⏱ 10.30am-5.30pm Mon-Thu, to 6pm Fri, to 4pm Sat Oct-Mar, to 3pm Sat Apr-Sep; 🚌 350S

Jan Frydendahl has been scouring the world for beautiful and quirky home design items for 30 years and his shop sells an eclectic and fascinating range of products; everything from chandeliers to watering cans spills out onto the pavement in front of his store.

GEORG JENSEN *Silver*
☎ 33 11 40 80; www.georgjensen.dk; Amagertorv 4; ⏱ 10am-6pm Mon-Thu, to 7pm Fri, to 5pm Sat, noon-4pm Sun; 🚌 350S; ♿

This is the world-famous silversmith's flagship store, selling everything from tiepins and watches, to silverware and gold pieces. It can be fearfully expensive but popular gifts for less than 300kr include candleholders and its iconic elephant bottle openers and key rings.

Trine Wackerhausen
Award-winning fashion designer

My fashion is inspired by… Architects such as Arne Jacobsen and Jørn Utzon, who fused minimalism with unique detailing and shapes. **Scandinavia's passion for minimalism stems from…** The cold weather. It's clean and crisp and makes the light and air very sharp. **The Copenhagen 'look' is…** Young women with long hair gathered in a bun, sailor T-shirts, leggings and wedges. This is what the city's legion of young fashion bloggers are wearing right now. There's also a lot of androgyny in Scandinavian fashion, which contrasts with southern Europe's more brazen, overtly sexual style. **When I'm not designing clothes…** I love relaxing in Assistens Kirkegård (p104). It's full of strange flowers, plants and old gravestones. For good music and a beer, I like Jolene Bar (p135), also good for checking out Copenhagen's more experimental fashion crowd.

STRØGET & AROUND

☐ HAY HOUSE
Homewares/Gifts
☎ 99 42 44 00; www.hay.dk; Østergade 61; ⏰ 11am-6pm Mon-Fri, to 4pm Sat; 🚌 350S

Rolf Hay's fabulous interior design store sells well-chosen examples of the latest Danish furniture as well as wonderful gifts, including Andreas Lintzer's cuddly towelling toys, books and homewares. Look out for their ceramic versions of plastic vending machine cups.

☐ HENRIK VIBSKOV *Fashion*
☎ 33 14 61 00; www.henrikvibskov .com; Krystalgade 6; ⏰ 11am-6pm Mon-Wed, to 7pm Thu & Fri, to 5pm Sat; Ⓜ Nørreport 🚉 S-train Nørreport 🚌 11, 6A

Not just a drummer and pro-lific artist (past exhibition venues include New York's PS1 MOMA), Danish enfant terrible Henrik Vibskov is pushing the fashion envelope, too. Stock up on his bold, multiprinted creations for progressive guys and girls, as well as other fashion-forward labels such as Surface to Air, Comme des Garçons and Walter Van Beirendonck.

☐ HOFF *Jewellery*
☎ 33 15 30 02; Kronprinsensgade 12; ⏰ noon-6pm Tue-Thu, to 7pm Fri, to 3pm Sat; 🚌 350S

Ingrid Hoff selects only the best Danish contemporary art jewellery for her showroom. Though her

Raise your style quotient with bold creations from Henrik Vibskov

designers mix gold and silver with acrylic and nylon, this is not just of-the-moment fashion jewellery but one-off and limited run pieces to last a lifetime.

ILLUMS BOLIGHUS
Homewares
☎ 33 14 19 41; www.royalshopping.com; Amagertorv 8-10; ☷ 10am-7pm Mon-Fri, to 5pm Sat, noon-5pm Sun; ᜑ 350S; ♿

If you only have time for one store in Copenhagen, this might well be the one. The Bolighus specialises in top-notch contemporary interior design, clothing, jewellery and furniture from big-name local and international designers. A little further east is its larger, sister department store, Illum.

LE KLINT *Homewares*
☎ 33 11 66 63; www.leklint.com; Store Kirkestræde 1; ☷ 10am-6pm Tue-Fri, to 4pm Sat; ᜑ 350S

These stunning handmade, concertina-style lampshades are works of art in themselves. Every Danish home boasts at least one of Klint's classic designs but their newer shades are every bit as interesting and rather more colourful.

LOUIS POULSEN *Homewares*
☎ 33 29 86 70; www.louispoulsen.com; Gammel Strand 28; ☷ 8am-4pm Mon-Thu, to 3.30pm Fri; ᜑ 350S

The new showroom of the famous Danish lighting brand, next to Thorvaldsens Hus on Gammel

Classic clothing for day or night at Day Birger Mikkelsen (p59)

Strand, offers state-of-the-art Scandinavian lighting design.

🔲 LUST *Erotica*
☎ 33 33 01 10; www.lust.dk; Mikkel Bryggers Gade 3A; 🕑 11am-7pm Mon-Thu, to 8pm Fri, to 6pm Sat; 🚍 6A, 12, 29, 33

Lust brings erotica into the mainstream, selling an eye-popping range of sex toys and videos. It is located just off Strøget and a long way – literally and spiritually – from grubby old Istedgade.

🔲 MAGASIN DU NORD
Department Store
☎ 33 11 44 33; www.magasin.dk; Kongens Nytorv 13; 🕑 10am-7pm Mon-Thu, to 8pm Fri, to 6pm Sat, noon-4pm Sun; M Kongens Nytorv 🚍 15, 19, 26, 1A; ♿

The best thing about this slightly old-fashioned but impressive department store – the oldest in Scandinavia, in fact – is its gourmet food hall in the basement. This is also where you will find the city's best range of international magazines.

🔲 MATAS *Health & Beauty*
☎ 33 14 07 85; www.matas.dk; Købmagergade 22; 🕑 10am-6pm Mon-Thu, to 7pm Fri, to 5pm Sat; 🚍 350S

Matas is a national chain of health and beauty stores (like Boots, but without the dispensing chemists), selling a wide range of vitamins, nonprescription medicines and

Need a magazine? Stop at Magasin du Nord

beauty products. This one, in the heart of Strøget, stocks products by the Danish skin-care guru, Ole Henriksen.

🔲 NORDISK KORTHANDEL
Books
☎ 33 38 26 38; Studiestræde 26; 🕑 10am-6pm Mon-Fri, 9.30am-3pm Sat; 🚍 10, 12, 14, 26, 29, 33

The best shop in the city for travel books and maps, mostly in English.

🔲 PETER BEIER *Food*
☎ 33 93 07 17; www.peterbeierchokolade .dk; Skoubogade 1; 🕑 10am-6pm Mon-Thu, to 7pm Fri, to 4pm Sat; 🚍 6A; ♿

The doyen of Copenhagen's booming artisanal chocolatier

scene. Small, but filled with hand-made chocolate treats.

POP CPH *Fashion*

☎ 33 12 00 04; www.popcph.dk; Grå-brødretorv 4; ⏰ 11am-6pm Mon-Thu, to 7pm Fri, 10am-5pm Sat; 🚌 6A

In 2005 Mikkel Kristensen and Kasper Henriksen began hosting parties for Copenhagen's creative community. The parties continue to inspire the duo's burgeoning fashion label: four collections per year combine dinner-party glamour with subversive detailing and hipster staples such as printed graphic tees.

ROYAL COPENHAGEN PORCELAIN *Homewares*

☎ 33 13 71 81; www.royalcopenhagen .com; Amagertorv 6; ⏰ 10am-6pm Mon-Thu, to 7pm Fri, to 5pm Sat, noon-5pm Sun; 🚌 350S; ♿

This is the main showroom for the historic Royal Danish Porcelain, one of the most popular souvenirs to take from a visit to the city since Nelson's time (legend has it he took some home after bombard-ing the city in 1807). Its 'blue fluted' pattern is famous around the world, as is its Flora Danica dinner service, costing upwards of a million kroner for a full set. The shop was recently refurbished and is definitely worth visiting even if you have no intention of buying anything.

RÜTZOU *Fashion*

☎ 33 32 63 20; www.rutzou.com; Store Regnegade 3; ⏰ 11am-5.30pm Mon-Thu, to 6pm Fri, to 4pm Sat; 🚌 350S

One of the leading names in contemporary Danish fashion, Susanne Rützou now has this im-pressive store in the city's fashion quarter. If you are searching for that kooky-feminine Copenhagen look, this is where you'll find it.

STILLEBEN *Ceramics*

☎ 33 91 11 31; www.stilleben.dk; Læderstræde 14, Strædet; ⏰ 11am-6pm Mon-Fri, to 4pm Sat; 🚌 6A

This tiny boutique is a favourite on the pedestrian street Strædet. Owners Ditte and Jelena are graduates of the Danish Design School's ceramic and glass course, and stock a contemporary and stunningly beautiful range of ceramic and glass from young, local designers.

STORM *Fashion*

☎ 33 93 00 14; Store Regnegade 1; ⏰ 11am-5.30pm Mon-Thu, 11am-7pm Fri, 10am-4pm Sat; 🚌 360S

Having recently graduated from the fashion 'underground' on Elmegade, this Danish fashion house now has a large corner store in the heartland of the city's fashion establishment. Storm sells an impressive range of Danish and international labels including

Famous Royal Copenhagen Porcelain on display

series of gourmet salads (think tomato and avocado with parsley, garlic, lime, chilli, red quinoa, and a trout oil and vinegar dressing). Liquid options include smoothies and freshly squeezed juices, including a strangely sublime spinach, apple and basil concoction. Your mama will be proud.

🍴 CAFÉ A PORTA *French* €€
☎ 33 11 05 00; www.cafeaporta.dk; Kongens Nytorv 17; 🕙 11am-midnight Mon-Thu, 11am-1am Fri, 10am-1am Sat, 10am-6pm Sun; Ⓜ Kongens Nytorv 🚌 1A, 15, 19, 26
Right by the metro station and next door to Magasin du Nord (p63), this magnificent Viennese cafe used to be a favourite of HC Andersen. It serves excellent, sizeable portions of classic brasserie food.

🍴 CAFÉ VICTOR *French* €€€
☎ 33 13 36 13; www.cafevictor.dk; Ny Østergade 8; 🕙 8am-1am Mon-Wed, to 2am Thu-Sat, 11am-midnight Sun; 🚌 350S
This classic French bar and brasserie is the doyen of the Copenhagen cafe scene and is enjoyably snobbish with jet-set pretensions and, generally, a more middle-aged crowd (regulation uniform: loafers, jeans and blazers for the men, Chanel for the women). The food is excellent, but a touch overpriced.

Visvim, Sixpack France and Anne Demeulemeester, as well as design books, CDs and fashion magazines.

🍴 EAT

🍴 42°RAW *Vegetarian* €€
☎ 32 12 32 10; www.42raw.com; Pilestræde 32; 🕙 8am-8.30pm Mon-Fri, 9am-6.30pm Sat, 10am-6.30pm Sun; 🚌 350S
The focus at hip and healthy 42°Raw is raw food, served in a

🍽 KRANSEKAGEHUS *Bakery*

☎ 33 13 19 02; Ny Østergade 9; ⏱ 10am-6pm Mon-Fri, to 4pm Sat; 🚌 350S

One of the best city-centre bakeries, Kransekagehuset specialises in the traditional marzipan cake known as *kransekage*.

🍽 LA GLACE *Cafe* €

☎ 33 14 46 46; Skoubougade 3-5; ⏱ 8.30am-5.30pm Mon-Fri, 8.30am-6pm Fri, 9am-5pm Sat; closed Sun; 🚌 6A

This enchanting cake and coffee shop next door to Peter Beier (p63) dates back to 1879. It serves some diet-busting sponge-mousse-cream concoctions, and the best hot chocolate in town.

🍽 POST & TELE MUSEUM CAFÉ *Danish* €€

☎ 33 41 09 86; www.cafehovedtelegrafen.dk; Købmagergade 37; ⏱ 10am-5pm Tue & Thu-Sat, to 8pm Wed, 11am-4pm Sun; Ⓜ Nørreport 🚉 S-train Nørreport; 🚻

This modern space does its best to bring the not overtly fascinating story of Post Danmark to life. The chief draw, however, is the excellent rooftop cafe, which serves a reasonable Danish-style lunch and has an outdoor terrace with fantastic views across the city centre to Christiansborg.

🍽 ROYAL CAFÉ *Danish* €€

☎ 33 13 71 81; www.theroyalcafe.dk; Amagertorv 6; ⏱ 10am-7pm Mon-Fri, to 6pm Sat, to 5pm Sun; 🚌 350S

Ceramic and glass items on display at Stilleben (p64)

In a courtyard to the right of Royal Copenhagen Porcelain (p64), this camp combo of pink paint and porcelain deer is famous for its dainty *smushi* (a sushi-smørrebrød hybrid). Combos include a very Danish salted beef with liver pâté.

🍽 SCHØNNEMANN *Danish* €€

☎ 33 12 07 85; www.restaurantschonnemann.dk; ⏱ 11.30am-5pm Mon-Sat; Ⓜ Nørreport 🚌 11, 350S

Schønnemann has been lining local bellies with smørrebrød (open sandwiches) and schnapps since 1877. Originally a hit with peasant farmers in town peddling their produce, its current fan base includes Michelin-lauded chefs and nostalgia-pining corporates. Not much else has changed, from the sawdust-sprinkled floors to the stoic Danish soul food. It's a local institution, so book ahead.

🍴 SLOTSKÆLDEREN HOS GITTE KIK
Danish   €

☎ 33 11 15 37; Fortunstræde 4; 11am-3pm Tue-Fri; 🚌 350S

This lunchtime smørrebrød restaurant is full of atmosphere and traditional Danish charm. Just point to the sandwich you want, and Gitte will prepare it and send it to your table.

🍸 DRINK

🍸 1105 *Cocktail Bar*

☎ 33 93 11 05; www.1105.dk; Kristen Bernikows Gade 4; 🕗 8pm-2am Wed, Thu & Sat, 4pm-2am Fri; Ⓜ Kongens Nytorv 🚌 11, 350S

Head in before 11pm for a bar seat at this luxe cocktail lounge. Domain of legendary barman Gromit Eduardsen, its perfect libations include the No 4 (Tanqueray gin, cardamom seeds, pepper, lime and honey). Whisky connoisseurs will be equally enthralled.

🍸 CAFÉ EUROPA *Cafe*

☎ 33 14 28 89; www.europa1989. dk; Amagertorv 1; 🕗 7.45am-11pm Mon-Thu, to 1am Fri & Sat, 9am-11pm Sun; 🚌 350S

Martin Hildebrandt, who runs this popular meeting place in the heart of the busy shopping area of Strøget, has won awards for his coffee, which he makes from his own special blend of home-roasted beans. This is one of the best places to watch Copenhagen go by, especially in summer when there is outdoor seating beside the elegant Storkspringvandet (stork fountain).

A MATTER OF TASTE

The Danes' usually unimpeachable good taste reveals its 'quirkier' side in some of their most popular foodstuffs:

> Pickled herring in curry sauce – Is this the most disturbing food combination ever?

> Salt liquorice – Do you eat it or leave it out for the slugs?

> *Remoulade* – A tart, celery-based mayonnaise. The Danes dollop it on everything, given half a chance.

> *Stegt flæsk med persille sovs* – A dish of pork fat, and nothing else, in parsley sauce. Mmmm.

> *Peberod* – Or 'horseradish', which the Danes cook to accompany meat, fish and everything else.

▼ JAILHOUSE CPH *Gay*

☎ 33 15 22 55; www.jailhousecph
.dk; Studiestræde 12; ☺ bar 3pm-2am
Sun-Thu, to 5am Fri & Sat, restaurant
Thu-Sat 6-11pm; ☐ 5A, 14, 173E, 6A

This two-storey, jail-themed
restaurant-bar is one of the most
popular venues on the Copenhagen gay scene.

▼ K-BAR *Cocktail Bar*

☎ 33 91 92 22; www.k-bar.dk; Ved
Stranden 20; ☺ 4pm-1am Mon-Thu, to
2am Fri & Sat; ☐ 350S

This laid-back lounge–cocktail bar
is tucked away behind Amagertorv. The 'K' stands for Kirsten,
who mixes a mean mojito to a
youngish, weekend-all-week and
preclub crowd.

▼ NEVER MIND *Gay*

www.nevermindbar.dk; Nørre Voldgade
2; ☺ 10pm-6am; ☐ 5A, 11, 14, 33

Tiny, smoky and packed to the
rafters, Never Mind is a seriously
fun spot for shameless pop and
late-night flirtation.

▼ RUBY *Cocktail Bar*

☎ 33 93 12 03; www.rby.dk; Nybrogade
10; ☺ 4pm-1am Mon-Wed, to 2am
Thu-Sat; ☐ 6A

Behind an unmarked door lies
one of Copenhagen's coolest
cocktail bars, where hipster-geek
mixologists shake whimsically
named drinks (an Importance of
Being Earnest, anyone?) and a
lively crowd spills into a labyrinth
of cosy, decadent rooms. For

Sample some *smushi* (a hybrid of sushi and smørrebrød) at the Royal Café (p66)

a gentlemen's club vibe, head downstairs (think Chesterfield lounges, oil paintings and wooden cabinets lined with spirits).

SPORVEJEN *Cafe/Bar*

☎ 33 13 31 01; Gråbrødretorv 17; 11am-11pm Mon-Sat, noon-11pm Sun; M Nørreport S-train Nørreport 6A

This tram-in-the-wall bar is rather tight on space (it is, literally, one of the old trams that used to run in the city), but has plenty of outdoor seating when weather permits. Great for a beer, not a bite.

ZIRUP *Cafe*

☎ 33 13 50 60; www.azhiba.dk; Læderstræde 32, Strædet; 10am-1am Mon-Thu, to 2am Fri-Sat; 6A;

This is one of the best cafe-restaurants on Strædet with a fresh and funky menu (burgers, Mexican, wraps, sandwiches and salads) to match its colourful, cosmopolitan interior design, but is also a great drinking spot when the sun goes down. There is plenty of outdoor seating during the summer – perfect for seeing and being seen.

ZOO BAR *DJ Bar*

☎ 33 15 68 69; www.zoobar.dk; Sværtegade 6; noon-midnight Tue & Wed, to 2am Thu, to 4am Fri & Sat; 350S

Zoo Bar is one of Copenhagen's favourite preclubbing hang-outs, pumping out anything from electronica to bop. Head in between

Zirup is ideal for a snack or a drink

9pm and 2am on Friday and Saturday nights for the best vibe.

PLAY

COPENHAGEN JAZZHOUSE *Live Music*

☎ 33 15 47 00; www.jazzhouse.dk; Niels Hemmingsensgade 10; vary; 6A, 350S

In just about any other city a venue as great as this would be horribly commercialised but Copenhagen's premiere jazz venue has a wonderfully unpretentious

Enter Café Europa to sample some of Copenhagen's best coffee (p67)

atmosphere that focuses on the music and performers. As well as some of the top names in the jazz world, you'll hear funk, blues, pop and, when the DJs get the downstairs dance floor heaving, an even wider range of contemporary music.

⭐ GRAND TEATRET *Cinema*

☎ 33 15 16 11; www.grandteatret. dk; Mikkel Bryggersgade 8; 🚊 Central Station, 🚌 5A, 6A, 11, 26, 30, 40
This attractive cinema, just off Strøget and close to Rådhus-

pladsen, is good for international art-house movies.

⭐ HUSET *Club/Bar/Cinema*

☎ 33 15 20 02; www.husetmagstraede .dk; Rådhusstræde 13; 🚌 6A, 11; ♿
This excellent arts centre is home to a variety of entertainment: Musik Cafeen, which promotes up-and-coming rock and pop acts; Salon K, which hosts mostly cabaret and chamber music; Planeten, home to experimental music and theatre; Underkanten, a venue for open-mic sessions and poetry slams; an art-house cinema; and

1.Sal, which shines the spotlight on jazz. And as if all this wasn't enough, there's a cafe and an Italian restaurant to boot. Admission and opening times vary.

⭐ JAZZHUS MONTMARTRE
Jazz

☎ **70 15 65 65; www.jazzhusmontmartre.dk; Store Regnegade 19A;** ☽ **noon-midnight Mon-Sat;** 🚌 **350S**

The reopening of Jazzhus Montmartre in 2010 signalled the rebirth of one of Scandinavia's great jazz venues. A contemporary cafe from noon to 8pm, the place gets back to its roots in the evenings, with live jams from both local and international talent. Recent guests include Australian jazz pianist Tom Vincent and French violin great Didier Lockwood. Check the website for upcoming performances.

⭐ KØBENHAVNS MUSIKTEATER *Theatre/Music*

☎ **33 32 38 30, tickets 33 32 55 56; www.kobenhavnsmusikteater.dk; Kronsprinsensgade 7;** 🚌 **350S**

Copenhagen's new avante-garde music and arts venue hosts a wide range of artistic crossover performances, exhibitions, hybrid art and talks. Admission and opening times vary.

⭐ LA FONTAINE *Jazz*

☎ **33 11 60 98; www.lafontaine.dk; Kompagnistræde 11, Strædet; admission varies;** ☽ **7pm-5am, live music 11pm-3am Fri & Sat, 9pm-1am Sun;** 🚌 **6A**

Copenhagen's oldest and cosiest jazz venue is right in the city centre. It offers live jazz from Friday to Sunday and is renowned for its late-night jam sessions.

>SLOTSHOLMEN

It might be small, but the 'island' of Slotsholmen has played a leading role in Copenhagen's history. It was here that Bishop Absalon founded a fortress in 1167, and it was around this fortress that Denmark's future capital city began to grow.

The fortress ruins lie beneath Christiansborg Slot, the mighty neo-baroque palace dominating Slotsholmen. Home of the Folketinget (Danish parliamentary chambers; p76), the palace complex harbours a number of cultural sights, including neoclassical Christiansborg Slotskirke (p74), whimsical De Kongelige Stalde & Kareter (p75) and the diva-adoring Teatermuseet (p77).

Drama defines Christiansborg Slot's own past. The stables and buildings surrounding the main courtyard date back to the 1730s when the original palace was built by Christian VI to replace a more modest model. Alas, the grander west wing of Christian VI's palace caught fire in 1794. Rebuilt in the early 19th century, it succumbed to flames once more in 1884. In 1907 the cornerstone for the third (and current) Christiansborg palace was laid by Frederik VIII.

Eight bridges connect Slotsholmen to the rest of the city, the most famous of which is Marmorbroen (the Marble Bridge), leading directly into Christiansborg Slot's rear courtyard.

SLOTSHOLMEN

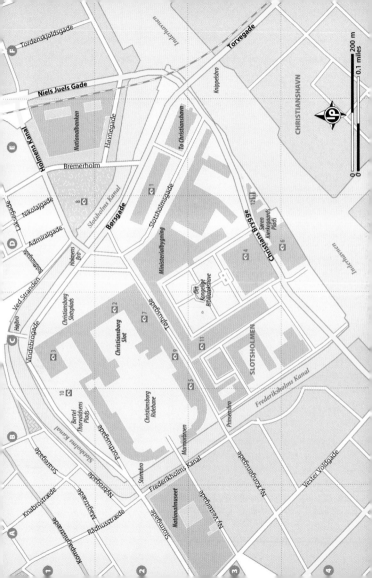

⊙ SEE

◎ BØRSEN

Børsgade; 🚌 1A, 2A, 40, 350S
The former stock exchange's ornate copper spire is made up of four dragons, their tails intertwining as they reach skywards to a height of 50m. It is one of the most striking landmarks in the city. The building still functions as a chamber of commerce but is rarely open to the public.

The twisting tailspin of Børsen's spire

◎ CHRISTIANSBORG RUINS

☎ 33 92 64 92; www.ses.dk; Christiansborg Slot; adult/child 40/20kr; 🕑 10am-4pm daily May-Sep, closed Mon Oct-Apr; 🚌 1A, 2A, 11, 40, 350S; ♿
In the cryptlike basement museum of Christiansborg you can see the ruins of Bishop Absalon's fortress, dating from 1167.

◎ CHRISTIANSBORG SLOTSKIRKE

Christiansborg Slotsplads; admission free; 🕑 noon-4pm Sun Jun-Aug, noon-4pm daily Jul; 🚌 1A, 2A, 11, 40, 350S; ♿
Tragedy struck CF Hansen's dignified neoclassical church (dating from 1826), next door to the parliament, on the day of the Copenhagen Carnival, 1992. A stray firework hit the scaffolding that had surrounded the church during a lengthy restoration and set the roof ablaze, destroying the dome. Miraculously, a remarkable frieze by Bertel Thorvaldsen that rings the ceiling just below the dome survived. The restorers went back to work and the church was reopened in January 1997.

◎ DANSK JØDISK MUSEUM

☎ 33 11 22 18; www.jewmus.dk; Kongelige Bibliotekshave (Royal Library garden); adult/child under 16yr/concession 50/free/40kr; 🕑 1-4pm Tue-Fri, noon-5pm Sat & Sun Sep-May, 10am-5pm Tue-Sun Jun-Aug; 🚌 1A, 2A, 11, 40, 66, 350S; ♿

Looking down on the grand Christiansborg Slot

Designed by Polish-born Daniel Libeskind, the Danish Jewish Museum is housed in an early-17th-century building (formerly the Royal Boat House) that has been transformed into an intriguing geometrical space. The museum's entrance is on the southern side of the garden, which lies to the rear of the Kongelige Bibliotek.

🎦 DE KONGELIGE STALDE & KARETER

☎ 33 40 10 10; www.kongehuset.dk; Christiansborg Ridebane 12; adult/child 20/10kr; 🕑 2-4pm Fri-Sun May-Sep, 2-4pm Sat & Sun Oct-Apr; 🚌 1A, 2A, 11, 40, 66, 350S

The Royal Stables & Coaches Museum has a unique collection of antique coaches, uniforms and riding paraphernalia, some of which is still used for royal occasions.

🎦 DET KONGELIGE BIBLIOTEK

☎ 33 47 47 47; www.kb.dk; Kierke-gaards Plads 1; admission free; 🕑 9am-9pm Mon-Fri, to 5pm Sat mid-Aug–Jun, 9am-7pm Mon-Fri, to 4pm Sat Jul–mid-Aug; 🚌 66, harbour bus; ♿

The Royal Library has two very distinct parts: the original, 19th-century red-brick building and the breathtaking granite-and-glass extension, completed in 1999. The latter, nicknamed the Black Diamond, is the main draw. People come simply to marvel at the interior with its giant glass wall and views across the harbour, or to enjoy a bite in the cafe or the minimalist Søren K restaurant (p77). You need to be a member to access what is the largest library in Scandinavia, containing 21 million books. Among them are original manuscripts and diaries by Kierke-gaard and Hans Christian Andersen (including the fairy-tale writer's

Granite and glass collide to form the Black Diamond, Det Kongelige Bibliotek (p75)

unsuccessful application to work at the library). The Black Diamond also hosts popular exhibitions and concerts. Check the website for details. To the rear of the library is Det Kongelige Bibliotekshave (the Royal Library garden), a pretty, leafy oasis in the heart of the city.

⊙ FOLKETINGET
☎ 33 37 55 00; www.ft.dk; Rigsdags-gården; admission free; ⊙ guided tours 2pm Mon-Fri & Sun Jul & Aug, 2pm Sun Sep-Jun; 🚌 1A, 2A, 11, 15, 65E; ⏦
The Danish parliamentary chamber is where 179 members of parliament debate national legislation and hold the government to account. Free tours in English at 2pm on Sundays and public holidays.

⊙ HOLMENS KIRKE
☎ 33 13 61 78; www.holmenskirke. dk; Holmens Kanal 9; admission free; ⊙ 10am-4pm Mon-Fri, 9am-noon Sat May-Sep, 10am-3pm Mon-Fri, 9am-noon Sat Oct-Apr; 🚌 1A, 2A, 11, 29, 350S
Not actually on Slotsholmen, but just across the canal that rings it to the northeast, the naval church was originally an anchor forge until being converted for worship in 1619. This is where many of Denmark's great seafaring heroes are buried, including Admiral Niels Juel, who defeated the Swedish fleet in the Battle of Køge Bay in 1677. Typical of Lutheran churches, the interior is spartan but notable for its carved, 17th-century oak altarpiece. Netto Boat canal tours

(p178) depart from here also. Dronning Margrethe and her consort Prince Henri were married here.

🅒 TEATERMUSEET

☎ 33 11 51 76; www.teatermuseet .dk; Christiansborg Ridebane 18; adult/child/concession 40/free/30kr; 🕑 11am-3pm Tue & Thu, to 5pm Wed, 1-4pm Sat & Sun; 🚌 1A, 2A, 11, 40, 66, 350S

Lovers of old theatres won't mind that the memorabilia in what used to be the Hofteater (Old Court Theatre) focuses, naturally, on Danish actors and productions. The theatre, which dates (in its current state) back to 1842, closed in 1881 but reopened as a museum in 1922. You can wander backstage, into the dressing rooms, and see the royal box, as well as examine old sets, costumes and posters.

🅒 THORVALDSENS MUSEUM

☎ 33 32 15 32; www.thorvaldsens museum.dk; Bertel Thorvaldsens Plads 2; adult/concession/child 20/10kr/free, free Wed, free audioguide; 🕑 10am-5pm Tue-Sun; 🚌 1A, 2A, 15, 65E; 🚻

One of the most distinctive buildings in Copenhagen, this colourful Greco-Roman mausoleum with its classically inspired friezes was the country's first purpose-built art museum. It houses the majority of works produced during the long and illustrious career of Bertel Thorvaldsen (1770–1844).

Thorvaldsen spent much of his working life in Rome, where he drew inspiration from classical mythology. The museum contains a fascinating collection of the artist's own collection of art and ancient artefacts from the Mediterranean region…and the artist himself, buried in the main room.

🅒 TØJHUSMUSEET

☎ 33 11 60 37; www.thm.dk; Tøjhusgade 3; adult/child/concession 30/free/15kr; 🕑 noon-4pm Tue-Sun; 🚌 1A, 2A, 11, 40, 66, 350S

The Royal Arsenal Museum houses a stunning collection of historic weaponry, from canons and medieval armour to pistols, swords and even a WWII flying bomb. Built by Christian IV in 1600, the 163m-long building is Europe's longest vaulted Renaissance hall.

🍴 EAT

🍴 SØREN K
Modern Danish €€€

☎ 33 47 49 49; www.soerenk.dk; Søren Kierkegaards Plads 1; 🕑 noon-midnight Mon-Sat; 🚌 47,66, harbour bus; 🚻

Bathed in light on even the dourest of days, the sleek, minimalist restaurant of the Black Diamond is one of the most stylish in the city. Its kitchen is dedicated to low-fat, light dishes made from strictly seasonal ingredients.

>NYHAVN TO KASTELLET

The colourful Dutch-style town houses that line the historic Nyhavn canal are one of the city's most photographed sights. Built in the 17th century to link the harbour to the city centre, today the canal is lined with popular, rather touristy bars and restaurants. On warmer, rain-free days, the cobbles are crowded with people downing a beer or two.

North of Nyhavn is Copenhagen's royal quarter, Frederiksstaden, where you will find the four palaces that make up Amalienborg Slot (p80) – the Danish royal family's main residence – as well as Marmorkirken (p82). Frederiksstaden stretches to Churchill Park, home to the Frihedsmuseet (p80) and the ancient city fortress, Kastellet (p81). Beside Kastellet, overlooking the harbour, is one of the city's most anticlimactic sights, the Little Mermaid (p82).

NYHAVN TO KASTELLET

SEE

AMALIENBORG SLOT

☎ 33 12 21 86; www.rosenborg-slot. dk; Amalienborg Plads; adult/child 60kr/ free, combined ticket incl Rosenborg Slot 100kr; ☼ 11am-4pm Tue-Sun Jan-Apr & Nov–mid-Dec, 10am-4pm May-Oct & mid-Dec–end Dec; ⊜ 1A, 15, 19; ♿

Amalienborg is made up of four rather staid 18th-century palaces ranged around a large cobbled square. It has been home to the Danish royal family since 1794. If you enter the square from the harbour to the east, the palace on your left is the home of the current queen, Margrethe II. Copenhagen's one great photo opportunity, the changing of the guard, takes place here every day at noon after the new guard has paraded through the city centre from its barracks beside Rosenborg Slot (p120). Across the square in another palace is the Amalienborg Museum, which recreates various royal rooms from the 19th century to WWII. The Danes are fervent royalists and love this kind of stuff, but this is perhaps not going to be of great interest to overseas visitors.

FRIHEDSMUSEET

☎ 33 47 39 21; www.natmus.dk; Churchillparken; admission free; ☼ 10am-3pm Tue-Sun Oct-Apr, to 5pm Tue-Sun May-Sep; ⊜ 1A, 15, 19, harbour bus Nordre Toldbod; ♿

MARGRETHE THE MARVELLOUS

One of the great paradoxes of this most democratic of societies is that its people are so un-questioningly devoted to their monarch. But Dronning Margrethe II is no ordinary monarch. She became queen – in the wake of a national referendum permitting women to succeed the throne – upon the death of her father in 1972 and was the first female Danish monarch since the 14th century. She is an undeniably excellent ambassador for the country, remains regal (unlike, say, the cycling Dutch royal family) and is a talented artist. Margrethe has illustrated a number of books, designed sets for the Royal Theatre and translated Simone de Beauvoir texts into Danish. She also chain-smokes, which is guaranteed to endear her to her compatriots. Her consort is the French-born Henrik, a mildly comic figure in Danish society. Together they have two children, the widely adored Crown Prince Frederik, who married a Tasmanian, Mary Donaldson, in 2004, and the slightly less loved Joachim (who divorced his Hong Kong–born wife, Alexandra, in the same year). Frederik and Mary remain the fairytale couple – dashing, beautiful and jetsetting – with many glamorous celebrity friends and an enviable life com-posed of foreign jaunts and sporting pleasures (both are keen sailors and horsey types). They have one son, Christian, and one daughter, affectionately named 'lille pige' (little girl) until her christening in July 2007. Europe's oldest monarchy looks to be in safe hands.

This small museum charts the exploits of the Danish resistance during the occupation by the Germans in 1940 to liberation by the British in 1945. Exhibits include moving letters written by resistance fighters awaiting execution, uniforms and sabotage equipment.

GALLERI CHRISTINA WILSON

☎ 32 54 52 06; www.christinawilson .net; Esplanaden 8B; ☺ noon-5pm Tue-Fri, to 3pm Sat, closed 3 weeks in Jul; 🚌 1A, 15, 20E

Arguably the most important commercial gallery in this district, Christina Wilson represents some of the world's most prolific contemporary artists. Top names include French conceptual artist and photographer Sophie Calle, American painter Michael Williams, and home-grown video artist Jesper Just.

KASTELLET

🚌 1A, 15, 19; ♿

The star-shaped fortress of Kastellet was originally commmissioned by Frederik III in 1662. Today it is one of the most historically evocative sites in the city. Its grassy ramparts and moat surround some beautiful 18th-century barracks, a chapel (sometimes used for concerts) and a tiny lifeguards museum (by the southern gate). On the ramparts is a historic windmill and some excellent views to

Vibrant textiles at Kunstindustrimuseet (p82)

the Little Mermaid, the harbour and, in the other direction, Marmorkirken.

KUNSTHAL CHARLOTTENBORG

☎ 33 13 40 22; www.kunsthalcharlot tenborg.dk; adult/concession 60/40kr; ☺ noon-8pm Tue-Fri, to 5pm Sat & Sun; Ⓜ Kongens Nytorv 🚌 1A, 11, 15, 19, 26; ♿

This large red-brick building is the historic home of the Kongelige Kunstakademi (Royal Academy of Fine Arts). It is one of the best venues to see contemporary Danish and international art, with changing exhibitions through the year.

THE LITTLE MERMAID

Love it or loathe it, when the world thinks of Copenhagen the statue of the Little Mermaid is the one of the first things that springs to mind. Unfortunately, many do seem to loathe this tiny statue of one of Hans Christian Andersen's most famous characters, which was created by sculptor Edvard Eriksen in 1913 and paid for by the Carlsberg Brewery. She has been vandalised repeatedly, losing her head and her arms on a couple of occasions. In 2006 Danish artist Bjørn Nørgaard was commissioned by Carlsberg (among others) to create a new Little Mermaid. He came up with a 'genetically altered' mermaid that sits not far from the original beside the harbour and is, in fact, probably truer in spirit to the rather bleak, twisted Andersen fairy tale. Unlike the Disney version, of course, Andersen's mermaid suffers all manner of physical and emotional torments, and definitely doesn't get her man.

☉ KUNSTINDUSTRIMUSEET

☎ 33 18 56 56; www.kunstindustri museet.dk; Bredgade 68; adult/child 60kr/free; ⏰ 11am-5pm Tue-Sun; ☐ 1A, 15, 19; ♿

The Danish Museum of Art and Design is one of the city's most stimulating cultural offerings, boasting an impressive collection of decorative arts, including extensive displays of European and oriental furniture, silverware and porcelain, with an emphasis on 20th-century Danish design. It's housed in a former hospital built around a courtyard in 1752. It's a wonderful spot to spend a rainy afternoon, and there is an inviting cafe to boot.

☉ MARMORKIRKEN

☎ 33 15 01 44; www.marmorkirken .dk; Frederiksgade 4; admission free, dome adult/child 25/10kr; ⏰ 10am-5pm Mon, Tue, Thu & Sat, to 6.30pm Wed, noon-5pm Fri & Sun, dome 1pm & 3pm Sat & Sun Sep–mid-Jun, 1pm & 3pm daily mid-Jun–Aug; ☐ 1A, 15, 19

The Marble Church, or to give it its correct name, Frederikskirken, is one of the most imposing pieces

Head for the imposing dome of Marmorkirken

Edvard Eriksen's waterside Little Mermaid statue

of architecture in the city and, we might add, a perhaps more fitting symbol for the Danish capital than the winsome Little Mermaid. Its dome was inspired by St Peter's in Rome and measures more than 30m in diameter. The original plans for the church were ordered by Frederik V and drawn up by Nicolai Eigtved. Construction began in 1749 but, as costs spiralled and the Danish economy foundered, the project was mothballed. It wasn't until Denmark's wealthiest financier, CF Tietgen, agreed to finance the church in the latter part of the 19th century that construction began again. You can climb up to the dome at

weekends; the views to Sweden are stunning. Do note that the church closes for weddings and funerals.

☑ MEDICINSK MUSEUM

☎ 35 32 38 00; www.museion.ku.dk; Bredgade 62; adult/concession 50/30kr; ⏱ guided tours 1.30pm, 2.30pm & 3.30pm Wed-Fri & Sun, English-language tours 2.30pm Jul & Aug; 🚌 1A, 15, 19

This fascinating, if occasionally gruesome, museum housed in a former teaching hospital covers the history of medicine, pharmacy and dentistry. It's all rather chilling, with plenty of pickled body parts and grisly diagrams. The original teaching theatre, where hundreds of cadavers have been dissected over the years, has an especially ghoulish atmosphere.

🛍 SHOP

The main areas of interest for shoppers here are stately Bredgade, which is home to the auction houses and high-end antique and art dealers; Store Kongensgade, which runs parallel to Bredgade to the north and has a broader range of independent shops and restaurants; and Store Strandstræde and Lille Strandstræde, which lie behind Nyhavn to the north and have several chic boutiques.

🎨 BANG & OLUFSEN
Electronics

☎ 33 11 14 15; www.bang-olufsen.com; Kongens Nytorv 26; ⏰ 10am-6pm Mon-Thu, to 7pm Fri, to 4pm Sat; Ⓜ Kongens Nytorv 🚌 1A, 15, 19, 26; ♿

The flagship store for the world-famous Danish audio-visual brand sells its distinctive, sleek, exquisitely designed TVs, stereos and other electrical equipment.

🎨 GALERIE ASBÆK *Art*

☎ 33 15 40 04; www.asbaek.dk; Bredgade 23; ⏰ 11am-6pm Mon-Fri, to 4pm Sat; Ⓜ Kongens Nytorv 🚌 1A, 11, 15, 19

Martin Asbæk has been at the centre of Copenhagen's contemporary art establishment for over 30 years and represents top local artists as well as some major names from overseas. He also sells slightly more affordable books and posters.

🎨 KERAMIK OG GLASVÆRKSTEDET *Ceramics*

☎ 33 32 89 91; www.keramikogglas vaerkstedet.dk; Kronprinsessegade 43; ⏰ noon-6pm Wed-Fri, 11am-2pm Sat; 🚌 26

Just off the tourist trail, this elegant gallery and studio show-cases the work of local ceramicists Ditte Fischer, Annemette Kissow, Sia Mai and Leif Hygild. Stock up on beautiful, organically shaped cups, vases and bowls.

🎨 KLASSIK MODERNE MØBELKUNST *Furniture*

☎ 33 33 90 60; www.klassik.dk; Bredgade 3; ⏰ 11am-6pm Mon-Fri, 10am-3pm Sat; 🚌 1A, 15, 19

This showroom, close to Kongens Nytorv, is the largest on Bredgade and features a trove of Danish de-sign classics from the likes of Poul Henningsen, Hans J Wegner, Arne Jacobsen, Finn Juhl and Nanna Ditzel – in other words, a veritable museum of Scandinavian furniture from the mid-20th century.

🎨 SUSANNE JUUL *Hats*

☎ 33 32 25 22; www.susannejuul .dk; Store Kongensgade 14; ⏰ 11am-5.30pm Tue-Thu, to 6pm Fri, to 2pm Sat; Ⓜ Kongens Nytorv 🚌 1A, 15, 19

BEST DESIGN STORES

> **Designer Zoo** (p130) – studio and showroom for local young designers
> **Illums Bolighus** (p62) – design superstore
> **Hay House** (p61) A candy store of designer furniture, textiles and must-have knick-knacks
> **Dansk Design Center** shop (p42) – excellent for design gifts
> **Klassik** (above) – Bredgade's one-stop shop for classic Danish design from the 20th century

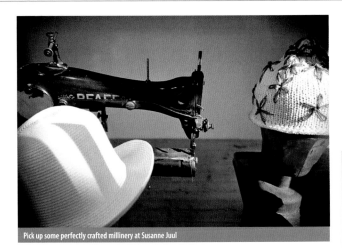

Pick up some perfectly crafted millinery at Susanne Juul

If you are looking for a hat that makes a statement, or something more discreet, this is the place to come. Perhaps the best milliners in the city, with prices ranging from 275kr to 5000kr.

⛏ EAT

⛏ 1.TH
Modern European/Danish €€€
☎ 33 93 57 70; www.1th.dk; Herluf Trolles Gade 9; ☺ invitation only, evenings Wed-Sat; Ⓜ Kongens Nytorv, ⓫ 1A, 11, 15, 19, 26
This unique, private dining 'restaurant' is housed in a classic Copenhagen apartment. 1.th translates as 'first floor, to the right' – the

location of this sumptuously decorated living and dining room, open to guests of chef Mette Martinussen. You reserve and pay the 1250kr bill (which includes wine) well in advance, then receive an invitation to a convivial, soirée-style evening with a multicourse dinner as the main attraction. Highly recommended, and the contemporary Danish-European food lives up to the high concept.

⛏ CAP HORN
Danish €€€
☎ 33 12 85 04; www.caphorn.dk; Nyhavn 21; ☺ 9am-1am (kitchen closes at 11pm); Ⓜ Kongens Nytorv ⓫ 1A, 11, 15, 26, 20E
Few places really stand out on Nyhavn but this is a perennial

favourite. Cap Horn is more refined than some of the other places here and serves accomplished Franco-Danish food with a good range of smørrebrød at lunch. There's an open fire in winter that turns the *hygge* (p154) meter up to '11'.

🍴 CUSTOM HOUSE
Global   €€€

☎ 33 31 01 30; www.customhouse.dk; Havnegade 44; ⏱ 11.30am–midnight Mon-Wed & Sun, to 1am Thu, to 2am Fri & Sat; 🚌 29, harbour bus Nyhavn; ♿
Sir Terence Conran's recently opened gourmet complex is housed in the old ferry terminal,

where boats used to embark for Sweden. As well as a small deli, there are three appealing upscale (or should that be 'Yuppies-cale'?) restaurants here. At **Bacino** the menu is contemporary but authentic Italian, with dishes including *langoustine* (shrimp) with pumpkin risotto or fillet of halibut with basil, courgette and almond cream. **Ebisu** serves what is for Copenhagen an unusually wide range of Japanese dishes, while the **Grill Bar** apes a more casual, upmarket New York steak joint. The food and service varies from excellent to so-so but, as you'd

Stop for a beer and smørrebrød at the refined Cap Horn (p85)

expect, the décor is smooth and sophisticated, with lots of dark stained wood and slate.

🍽 DAMINDRA *Japanese* €€€
☎ 33 12 33 75; www.damindra.dk; Holbergsgade 26; 🕙 11am-10pm Tue-Sat; 🚌 11, 29

Soothing interiors, a knowledge-able staff and unforgettable Japanese dishes define this little-known gem. The owner, Damindra, designed just about everything you see, including the cutlery, glasses and the chair you're sitting on. Most importantly, his pride and passion are reflected in the food his Japanese chefs prepare: from the buttery sashimi to an un-forgettable prawn tempura, it's all obscenely fresh, flavoursome and beautifully presented. The 'Chef's Choice' set sushi menu (368kr) provides the perfect culinary tour, while desserts such as chocolate brûlée with Earl Grey ice cream make for a wicked epilogue. Cap it all off with a complimentary *soju* and plum wine 'espresso'.

🍽 EMMERYS *Bakery* €
☎ 33 93 01 33; www.emmerys.dk; Store Strandstræde 21; 🕙 8am-6pm Mon-Thu, 7.30am-6.30pm Fri, 8am-5pm Sat & Sun; 🚌 1A, 11, 15, 19; 🚭

This sophisticated, trendy bakery, coffee shop and delicatessen chain has branches throughout Copen-hagen (in Nørrebro, Vesterbro and Østerbro) selling its own brand of coffee, as well as cakes, muffins, bread, wine and chocolate. Irresist-ible and high up on the list of locals' favourites for a weekend treat.

🍽 LE SOMMELIER *French* €€€
☎ 33 11 45 15; www.lesommelier.dk; Bredgade 63; 🕙 noon-2pm & 6-10pm Mon-Thu, noon-2pm & 6-11pm Fri, 6-11pm Sat, 6-10pm Sun; 🚌 1A, 15, 26

A chic, pared-back combo of white linen tables, wooden floorboards and vintage French and Italian posters, Le Sommelier is a good spot for midrange gourmet feast-ing. Here, French traditions meet seasonal Nordic produce, creating memorable dishes such as Norwe-gian lobster with lobster bisque and crab salad. Flavours are clean and comforting, and the wine list has a particularly impressive French selection. Book ahead.

🍽 OFELIA *Danish* €€€
☎ 33 69 39 31; www.kglteater .dk; Skuespilhuset (Royal Danish Playhouse), Sankt Annæ Plads 36; 🕙 11am-9pm Mon-Sat; 🚌 11, 29, harbour bus Nyhavn

Waterfront views, al fresco tables and fresh Nordic flavours: Ofelia's popularity is no surprise. Located inside Skuespilhuset (p91), it's also a fabulous place to chill with a passionfruit martini.

Toke Lykkeberg
Art critic, curator & co-director of IMO Gallery (see p129)

For the art scene low-down… Scan www.kopenhagen.dk. **Copenhagen's art world is…** Divided into three main precincts. The first, centred on Bredgade and Store Kongensgade, is crammed with major commercial galleries, including Galleri Christina Wilson (p81). In Vesterbro, Kødbyen (Meatpacking District) is home to street-art favourite V1 Gallery (p129) and the more classical Galleri Bo Bjerggaard. Further west is new hot spot Ny Carlsberg Vej 68 (p129). **Contemporary local talent includes…** Conceptual artists Olafur Eliasson (creator of the 2008 New York City Waterfalls project), Jeppe Hein and Elmgreen & Dragset. Tal R creates colourful figurative paintings bordering on abstract, and designer Henrik Vibskov is famous for his outrageous catwalk shows. Social art group Superflex has produced everything from a create-your-own-gas system in Africa to affordable copies of Danish furniture pieces. **Don't miss…** Ny Carlsberg Glyptotek (p42) for Manet, the biggest Rodin collection outside France and an amazing Winter Garden.

🍽 RESTAURANT AOC
Modern Danish €€€

☎ 33 11 11 45; www.premisse.dk; Dronningens Tværgade 2; ⏱ 6-10pm Tue-Sat; Ⓜ Kongens Nytorv 🚌 1A , 11, 15, 19,

A sublime culinary experience is guaranteed in this vaulted cellar restaurant in a historic mansion. Chefs Ronny Emborg and Michael Munk take the sourcing of the finest Danish ingredients for their restaurant very seriously, applying classic French techniques, learned during stints at Michelin restaurants, with dedication and wit. Meanwhile, sommelier Christian Aarø Mortensen is a champion wine steward with an exceptional list (it's particularly strong on French wines).

🍽 RESTAURANT D'ANGLETERRE
Danish/French €€€

☎ 33 37 06 45; www.dangleterre.dk; Hotel d'Angleterre, Kongens Nytorv 34; ⏱ 7am-10pm Sun-Thu, to 11pm Fri & Sat; Ⓜ Kongens Nytorv 🚌 1A , 11, 15, 19, 26

Copenhagen's hotel restaurants are not usually terribly appealing, but the five-star Hotel d'Angleterre's is a cut above, serving alluring Franco-Danish cuisine built upon a solid foundation of the best Danish raw ingredients, and served in a glamorous, glistening dining room overlooking Copenhagen's grandest square.

🍽 SALT
Modern Danish/French €€€

☎ 33 74 14 44; www.saltrestaurant .dk; Toldbodgade 24-28; ⏱ noon-4pm & 5-10pm; 🚌 29; ♿

A converted 18th-century corn warehouse is the beautiful venue for this Terence Conran–designed (yes, him again) Modern Danish–French hotel restaurant close to the site of the new theatre. Seafood, local organic meats and game are regulars on an ambitious menu that might include confit of monkfish, crisp fried crab with pomegranate or roast rack of rabbit.

🍽 TASTE *French Cafe* €

☎ 33 93 77 97; www.tastedeli.eu; Store Kongensgade 80-82; ⏱ 9.30am-6pm Mon-Fri, 10am-6pm Sat & Sun; 🚌 1A, 15, 19; ♿

Just around the corner from Marmorkirken is this delectable French-owned deli-takeaway-cafe serving mostly organic, homemade cakes, bread, salads, chocolates and salad along with the best muffins in Copenhagen.

🍽 WOKSHOP CANTINA
Asian €

☎ 33 91 61 21; www.wokshop.dk; Ny Adelgade 6; ⏱ noon-2pm, 5.30-10pm Mon-Fri, 6-10pm Sat; Ⓜ Kongens Nytorv 🚌 1A ,11, 15, 19, 26

This great-value, Wagamama-style modern Thai place is close to

DRINK

PALÆ BAR *Pub*
☎ 33 12 54 71; Ny Adelgade 5;
🕐 11am-1am Mon-Wed, to 3am Thu-Sat, 4pm-1am Sun; Ⓜ Kongens Nytorv
🚍 1A, 11, 15, 19, 26

This cosy, old-school drinking den is popular with an older crowd of journalists, writers and politicians.

UNION BAR *Cocktail Bar*
☎ 41 19 69 76; www.theunionbar.dk; Store Strandstræde 19; 🕐 8pm-2am Wed & Thu, 4pm-3am Fri, 8pm-3am Sat;
🚍 1A, 11, 15, 20E

THE HOMES OF HANS CHRISTIAN ANDERSEN

Despite earning great wealth in later life, Hans Christian Andersen never owned his own home but instead rented apartments at three addresses on Nyhavn during his life – first at No 20, where he began writing the stories that would make him world famous, then for 17 years at No 67 and finally at No 18. This restless traveller, who journeyed as far as Istanbul and North Africa and whom many believe was homosexual, loved to watch the life of the canal and feel as if he were in touch with the world across the sea. Although the sailors down below might also have been part of the appeal… (see also p45).

Inspired by the speakeasy bars of old New York (even the cocktails are named after 1920s slang), the Union hides away behind an unmarked black door. To enter, ring the buzzer and head down the stairs to a suitably dim, decadent scene of handsome bartenders, in-the-know revellers and smooth jazz and blues tunes.

PLAY

DET KONGELIGE TEATER (THE ROYAL THEATRE) *Theatre*
☎ 33 69 69 69; www.kglteater.dk; Kongens Nytorv; Ⓜ Kongens Nytorv 🚍 1A, 11,15, 19, 26; ♿

With theatre productions moved to the harbour-front Skuespilhuset (p91) and opera transferred to the striking new Opera House (p100), the historic Gamle Scene ('old stage') on Kongens Nytorv now focuses primarily on world-class productions from the Royal Danish Ballet. The current building, the fourth theatre to occupy the site, was completed in 1872 and was designed by Vilhelm Dahlerup and Ove Petersen. The statues by the steps are of Ludvig Holberg, the 18th-century playwright, and Adam Oehlenschläger, the national poet. If you're a dance fiend with a thirst for a bargain, hit the theatre's **box office** (☎ 33 69 69 69; August Bournonvilles Passage 1; 🕐 2-6pm Mon-Sat) from 6pm on the day of

Statue of the national poet at Det Kongelige Teater

Brainchild of promoters Simon Frank and Simon Lennet, this is the city's new 'It' club. Occupying a former art gallery, its biggest (and smallest) claims to fame are A-list DJ talent and dwarves behind the bar. Expect selective electronica and an even more selective door policy (Fridays are more accessible than Saturdays). If you have a Danish SIM card, register for updates online.

⭐ SKUESPILHUSET (ROYAL DANISH PLAYHOUSE) *Theatre*
☎ 33 69 69 69; www.kglteater.dk; Sankt Annæ Plads 36; admission varies, 50-710kr, 50% discount under 25s & over 65s; 🚌 11, 29, harbour bus Nyhavn; ♿ Designed by Boje Lundegaard and Lene Tranberg, Copenhagen's striking playhouse is home to the Royal Danish Theatre and a world-class repertoire of both homegrown and foreign plays (recent productions have included Ludvig Holberg's classic *Jeppe of the Hill* and Sarah Kane's 'in-yer-face' *4:48 Psychosis*). Tickets often sell out well in advance but any unsold go for half-price at the **box office** (☎ 33 69 69 69; 🕐 noon-8pm) from 6pm on the day of the performance.

a performance when any unsold tickets are offered at half-price.

⭐ SIMONS *Club*
☎ 53 38 90 03; www.simonscopen hagen.com; Store Strandstræde 14; 🕐 Fri & Sat; 🚌 1A, 11, 15, 19

>CHRISTIANSHAVN & ISLANDS BRYGGE

Historic canals, quirky churches, 18th-century town houses and leafy city ramparts combine to make Christianshavn one of Copenhagen's prettiest quarters. This is mostly a residential area, home to not-really-struggling artists, yuppies doing their best to look relaxed and bohemian, and a large Greenlandic community. Slap-bang in the middle of it all, like some quarrelsome, elderly relative whom everyone tries to ignore, is Christiania (p94), the 'alternative community' founded in an army barracks in 1971. Further northeast of here is Holmen, formerly a naval base and industrial area, now home to the Danish Film and Architecture schools, costly waterside apartments and the magnificent new Opera House (p100).

On the other side of Amager Boulevard from Christianshavn, to the south, is one of Copenhagen's upcoming areas, Islands Brygge, which has a striking harbour swimming pool (p100). Islands Brygge really comes alive during the summer when it serves as a kind of inner-city beach, albeit one without sand. Come here in the winter, however, and you might wonder what all the fuss is about…

CHRISTIANSHAVN & ISLANDS BRYGGE

◉ SEE
Christiania Entrance 1 C3
Christians Kirke 2 B4
Gammel Dok 3 C3
Overgaden 4 C3
Vor Frelsers Kirke 5 C3

⑪ EAT
Aristo 6 B4
Bastionen og Løven 7 C4
Café Wilder 8 C3

Lagkagehuset 9 C4
Morgenstedet 10 D3
Noma 11 C3
Spiseloppen 12 C3
Sweet Treat 13 C3
Tobi's Café 14 B5
Viva 15 B4

▾ DRINK
Sofie Kælderen 16 C4

★ PLAY
Copenhagen Opera
House 17 D2
Islands Brygge
Havnebadet 18 A4
Koncerthuset 19 C6
Loppen .... (see 12)

SEE

CHRISTIANIA

☎ 32 95 65 07; www.christiania.org; Prinsessegade; Ⓜ Christianshavn ⛟ 66

The dream of a self-sufficient, utopian society rooted in the free love and chemical indulgence of the late 1960s has turned sour in recent years. The police have clamped down on the open sale of soft drugs but drug-related violence has actually increased since, and there appears to be quite an alcohol problem here. But the sheer 'otherness' of the Christiania lifestyle guarantees an eye-opening experience for visitors, nonetheless. The main entrance is located on Prinsessegade, 200m northeast of its intersection with Bådmandsstræde. There is a small market selling the usual market tat on the right, as well as a couple of cafe-restaurants and genuine craftspeople elsewhere on the site. You can take a guided tour of Christiania with a local resident. Tours meet inside the main entrance at 3pm on weekends (daily in July and August). See also p12.

CHRISTIANS KIRKE

☎ 32 54 15 76; Strandgade 1, admission free; ☯ 10am-4pm Tue-Sun; Ⓜ Christianshavn ⛟ 2A, 19, 47, 66, 350S, harbour bus Knippelsbro

Nicolai Eigtved's theatre-like church was completed in 1759.

WORTH THE TRIP

Amager Strandpark (Ⓜ Amager Strand) is a sand-sational artificial lagoon, 10 minutes from Christianshavn on the coast road to the airport. A popular water-sports destination, it offers summertime bars and cafes, and impressive views of Øresund Bridge.

If swimming comes third to cabanas and cocktails, head to glam 'beach club' **Halvandet** (☎ 70 27 02 96; www.halvandet.dk; Refshalevej 325; ☯ end Apr–mid-Sep; ⛴ harbour bus Halvandet; ⛟ 40, then 30-minute walk). On the northern tip of Holmen, 1.5km north of the Opera House, it's *the* place to tan, nosh and gaze at the skyline (or gym-fit talent).

Twenty minutes north of Copenhagen, at the heart of the 'Danish Riviera', small but pristine **Bellevue Beach** (⛟ S-train Klampenborg) also throngs with summertime body-beautifuls. Compromise your figure at excellent Franco-Danish restaurant **Den Gule Cottage** (☎ 39 64 06 91; www.dengulecottage.dk; Strandvejen 506, Klampenborg; ☯ noon-5pm, & 6-10pm Sun-Thu, to midnight Fri & Sat; ⛟ S-train Klampenborg), located on the hill overlooking the beach.

Further afield, virtually the entire Zealand north coast is made up of time-warped fishing villages and sandy beaches, two of the best being Gilleleje and Hornbæk (both reachable by train from Helsingør).

Christianshavn's art is not just restricted to its galleries

This is a frequent venue for classical music recitals (leaflets at the entrance to the church provide details).

GAMMEL DOK

☎ 32 57 19 30; www.dac.dk; Strandgade 27B; exhibition adult/concession/child 40/25kr/free; 🕙 10am-5pm Thu-Tue, to 9pm Wed; Ⓜ Christianshavn 🚌 2A, 19, 47, 66, 350S; &

Home to the Dansk Arkitektur Center, this converted 19th-century warehouse offers changing exhibitions on Danish and international architecture, as well as an excellent bookshop.

OVERGADEN

☎ 32 57 72 73; www.overgaden.org; Overgaden Neden Vandet 17; admission free; 🕙 1-5pm Tue, Wed & Fri-Sun, 1-8pm Thu; Ⓜ Christianshavn 🚌 2A, 19, 47, 66, 350S,

Rarely visited by tourists, this tucked-away gallery mounts challenging exhibitions of contemporary installation art and photography, usually by younger artists.

COPENHAGEN FOR FREE

Copenhagen has a reputation for being a costly city, but many of its top sights are free for at least one day of the week. The following items are free all week unless a particular day is specified.

> **Assistens Kirkegård** (p104)
> **Christiania** (p94)
> Churches, including **Marmorkirken** (p82) and **Vor Frelsers Kirke** (below)
> **Davids Samling** (p118)
> **Den Hirschsprungske Samling** (free on Wednesday only; p118)
> **Folketinget** (p76)
> **Frihedsmuseet** (p80)
> **Kastellet** (p81)
> **Københavns Bymuseet** (free on Friday only; p128)
> **Little Mermaid** (p82)
> **Nationalmuseet** (p42)
> **Ny Carlsberg Glyptotek** (free on Sunday only; p42)
> **Ny Carlsberg Vej 68** (p129)
> **Statens Museum for Kunst** (p120)
> **Thorvaldsens Museum** (free on Wednesday only; p77)
> **Tøjhusmuseet** (free on Wednesday only; p77)

⊙ VOR FRELSERS KIRKE (CHURCH OF OUR SAVIOUR)

☎ 32 57 27 98; Sankt Annæ Gade 29; admission free, tower adult/child 25/10kr; ☯ church 11am-3.30pm, tower 11am-4pm; Ⓜ Christianshavn ⊞ 2A, 19, 47, 66, 350S

The extraordinary spire is the main draw at this 17th-century church close to Christiania (p94). It takes a strong resolve to climb all the way to the top, 400 steps and 95m up, as the last 150 steps run around the *outside* of the tower, narrowing to the point where they literally disappear. The tower was added to the church in 1752 by

Lauritz de Thurah, who took his inspiration from Boromini's tower of St Ivo in Rome.

🍴 EAT

🍴 ARISTO
Mediterranean €€

☎ 32 95 83 30; www.cafearisto.dk; Islands Brygge 4; ☯ 11am-midnight Mon-Thu, 11-2am Fri, 10-2am Sat, 10am-11pm Sun; ⊞ 5A, 12, 33, 34, 40, 250S; ♿

At the heart of pulsating Islands Brygge is this airy, contemporary cafe-restaurant serving pretty, modern Danish and fusion cuisine such as *quail pot au feu* (gently

René Redzepi
Head chef, Noma (see p99)

Nordic cuisine is about... A sense of time and place, purity, nature, commitment, patience and determination. I find inspiration in Nordic landscapes, memories, and conversations between growers, colleagues and people living in nature. **A lesser-known local ingredient...** Is sea arrow-grass, a plant we pick on the shores of Zealand. It's a succulent and tastes like coriander. **My Macedonian heritage...** Helps me see different contexts for local produce and cooking techniques. For many native Danes, certain foods and methods had only been seen in one specific light. **Foodies in Copenhagen shouldn't miss...** Eating traditional Danish smørrebrød (open sandwiches) at Schønnemann (p66) and fresh fish at Kødbyens Fiskebar (p132) **I will never again...** Put soil in my mouth. I tasted it on one of my foraging trips

simmered quail), or *pork tenderloin saltimbocca* (filled pork rolls).

🍴 BASTIONEN OG LØVEN
Danish €€€

☎ 32 95 09 40; www.bastionen-loven .dk; Christianshavns Voldgade 50; 10am-midnight; 🚌 2A, 19, 47, 66, 350S

This charming cafe-restaurant is housed beside a historic windmill on the city ramparts just south of Christiania. Its front garden is the perfect place to enjoy a classic Copenhagen brunch – cheese, smoked salmon, omelette, pancakes, fresh fruit, yoghurt, bacon, coffee, juice etc – on a sunny Sunday morning.

🍴 CAFÉ WILDER *Cafe* €€

☎ 32 54 71 83; Wildersgade 56; 🕐 9am-midnight Mon, 9am-1am Tue & Wed, 9am-2am Thu & Fri, 9.30-2am Sat, 9.30am-midnight Sun; Ⓜ Christianshavn 🚌 2A, 19, 47, 66, 350S; ♿

This friendly, laid-back corner cafe in the heart of Christianshavn serves simple, beautiful dishes such as goat cheese au gratin on bruschetta, and roasted cockerel breast with butter-sautéed asparagus, pak choi and baby carrots. One of Copenhagen's oldest cafes, it's popular with local bohemians.

🍴 LAGKAGEHUSET *Bakery* €

☎ 32 57 36 07; www.lagkagehuset.dk; Torvegade 45; 🕐 6am-7pm Mon-Fri, to 6pm Sat & Sun; Ⓜ Christianshavn 🚌 2A, 19, 47, 66, 350S; ♿

This much-loved bakery – recently voted the best in the city – sells excellent sandwiches as well as the usual sticky, sweet pastries and heavyweight rye bread.

🍴 MORGENSTEDET
Vegetarian €

Langgade, Christiania; 🕐 noon-9pm Tue-Sun; Ⓜ Christianshavn 🚌 66

A homely, hippy little place in the heart of the alternative commune of Christiania, Morgenstedet offers but one dish of the day, always veg-

WHEN IS A DANISH NOT A DANISH

Wherever you go in Denmark the bakeries tend to stock the same range of syrupy, buttery, nut-sprinkled pastries with perhaps a dab of jam or custard in the middle. To the rest of the world they are known as 'Danish pastries', but ask for 'a Danish' in a *bageri* in Copenhagen and the baker will probably give you a funny look and perhaps direct you to the brothels of Istedgade. The Danes call them *wienerbrød* (literally 'Vienna bread') and, true to their collective sweet tooth, they eat them for breakfast. A quick look in the history books tells us that *wienerbrød* is the more appropriate name as this style of cake originated in Austria in the 18th century.

etarian, mostly organic, usually a curry and always at a bargain price.

🍴 NOMA
Modern Nordic €€€

☎ 32 96 32 97; www.noma.dk; Strandgade 93; ⏱ noon-1.30pm & 6-10pm Tue-Sat; 🚌 2A, 19, 47, 66, 350S; ♿

Topping the S Pellegrino 'World's Best Restaurants' list in 2010, this Michelin-starred restaurant is the domain of chef René Redzepi (formerly of Le Bulli and the French Laundry). The menu features only Scandinavian-sourced produce such as musk ox, *skyr* curd and locally caught seafood, transformed into extraordinary New Nordic creations, including octopus legs with sorrel stems, sloe, blackberries and egg yolk. Book three months ahead.

🍴 SPISELOPPEN
Global €€

Langgade, Christiania; ☎ 32 57 95 58; www.spiseloppen.dk; ⏱ 5-10pm Tue-Sun; Ⓜ Christianshavn 🚌 66

This ambitious dinner restaurant situated in the Loppen building serves up a global menu – the cuisine depends on the nationality of the kitchen's chef on the night!

🍴 SWEET TREAT *Cafe* €

☎ 32 95 41 15; www.sweettreat.dk; Sankt Annæ 3A; ⏱ 7.30am-7pm Mon-

Docked for a dinner at Noma

Fri, 10am-6pm Sat & Sun; Ⓜ Christianshavn 🚌 2A, 19, 66, 350S

Effortlessly cool with its strung light bulbs, hipster mags and turntable (feel free to choose a disc to play), this intimate local cafe peddles brilliant coffee and seasonally inspired smoothies (soy milk available!). Breakfast options include oatmeal, while the freshly made smørrebrød (open sandwiches) are a digestible 28kr. The fish-ball sandwich, with chopped cucumber and homemade remoulade, is especially good.

TOBI'S CAFÉ *Cafe* €

☎ 88 38 80 83; Leifsgade 3; ⏱ 8am-7pm Mon-Thu, 8am-midnight Fri, 10am-midnight Sat, 10am-5pm Sun; Ⓜ Islands Brygge

This local favourite peddles good coffee, flaky pastries and savoury nosh such as eggs with rye, cheese and salami.

VIVA *Global* €€

☎ 27 25 05 05; www.restaurantviva.dk; Langebrogade Kajplads 570; ⏱ 11.30am-3pm & 5.30pm-midnight Mon-Thu, 11.30am-3pm & 5.30pm-1am Fri & Sat, 5.30-9pm Sun; 🚌 5A, 12, 33, 40, 250S

This unique restaurant, on board a ship moored beside Langebro, has the same team behind Aura and a similarly inventive menu of tapas-sized, modern European dishes.

DRINK

SOFIE KÆLDEREN
DJ/Jazz Bar

☎ 32 57 77 01; www.sofiekaelderen .dk; Over Gaden Oven Vandet 32; ⏱ 11.30am-midnight Mon-Wed, 11am-3am Thu-Sat, 11am-10pm Sun; Ⓜ Christianshavn 🚌 2A, 19, 47, 66, 350S

This former old-school jazz bar in a cellar beside the canal is now a cool live-music venue and lounge, serving globally influenced food for lunch and dinner.

PLAY

COPENHAGEN OPERA HOUSE *Live Music*

Box office ☎ 33 69 69 69; www.kgl teater.dk; Ekvipagemestervej 10; tickets 375-895kr, standing seats 115kr, 50% discount under 25s & over 65s; ⏱ vary; 🚌 66, harbour bus Operaen; ♿

This state-of-the-art opera house features two stages, the Main Stage and a smaller venue, Takkeløftet. The repertoire runs the gamut from classic to contemporary opera, as well as the odd curve ball like a performance by Elvis Costello or something from the Jazz Festival (p21). Productions usually sell out way in advance but any unsold tickets are offered at half-price at the Opera House box office from 6pm on the night of the performance. Alternatively, many come just to eat in the panoramic Franco-Danish restaurant or the ground-floor cafe, or to explore the building on a guided tour. The tours run Saturdays and Sundays at 9.30am and 4.30pm (100kr).

ISLANDS BRYGGE HAVNEBADET *Swimming*

☎ 23 71 31 89; Islands Brygge, beside Langebro; admission free; ⏱ 7am-7pm Mon-Fri, 11am-7pm Sat & Sat Jun-Aug; 🚌 5A, 12, 33, 34, 40, 250S

This has to be the funkiest public swimming pool (designed

Opera lovers flock to the Copenhagen Opera House

by trendy architects Plot) you'll ever see. It takes some courage to plunge into the waters of Copenhagen harbour, though they do at least test it regularly for cleanliness. If you don't fancy a swim, there are lawns, skateboarding parks, basketball courts, restaurants and cafes where you can chill out on a sunny day. It has a real carnival atmosphere during the summer holidays.

☆ KONCERTHUSET Live Music
☎ 35 20 30 40; www.dr.dk/Koncert huset/; Emil Holms Kanal 20; Ⓜ Universitetet, 🚌 33, 77, 78; ♿

Home of the National Symphony Orchestra, Jean Nouvel's bold blue 'Concert House' hosts everything from classical tunes to jazz, pop and experimental.

☆ LOPPEN Live Music
☎ 32 57 84 22; www.loppen.dk; Christiania; ⏱ 9pm-2/3am; admission varies free-240kr; Ⓜ Christianshavn 🚌 66
This historic, timbered warehouse in Christiania doesn't draw quite so many major international acts as it used to but is still one of the best live-music venues in the city – everything from punk to reggae, funk and world music can be heard here, usually followed by a boisterous disco into the early hours.

>NØRREBRO & ØSTERBRO

Nørrebro and Østerbro are chalk-and-cheese neighbours: one cool, lively, ethnically diverse and edgy, the other sedate, family-oriented and a little smug. Nørrebro started off as a working-class neighbourhood and now has a large immigrant community. As well as hosting the occasional riot (the most recent example being the violent and prolonged demonstration against the closing of a well-established squat, Ungdomshuset, in March 2007), Nørrebro is one of the most delectable nightlife destinations in the city and it is also a cutting-edge fashion centre.

Østerbro, or the 'embassy quarter', has some good midrange shopping, restaurants and the city's largest park, Fælledparken (p105), home to the national stadium, Parken (p115).

Nørrebro and Østerbro lie to the northwest and northeast of the city centre respectively, stretching from the eastern Vesterbro–Frederiksberg border to Nordhavn, the northern harbour.

NØRREBRO & ØSTERBRO

◉ SEE

🏠 SHOP

🍴 EAT

🍸 DRINK

⭐ PLAY

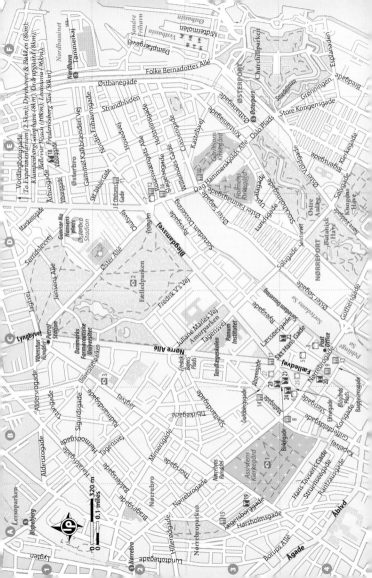

SEE

ASSISTENS KIRKEGÅRD

☎ 35 37 19 17; Kapelvej 4, Nørrebro; admission free; ◷ 8am-4pm Nov-Feb, to 6pm Mar, Apr, Sep & Oct, to 8pm May-Aug; 🚌 5A, 350S; &

This leafy cemetery in the heart of Nørrebro is the burial place of some of Denmark's most celebrated citizens including Hans Christian Andersen, his old foe Søren Kierkegaard and physicist Niels Bohr. The main entrance is on Kapelvej. You should be able to pick up a map at the office here.

EXPERIMENTARIUM

☎ 39 27 33 33; www.experiment arium.dk; Tuborg Havnevej 7, Hellerup; admission adult/child under 2yr/3-11yr 148/free/97kr; ◷ 9.30am-5pm Mon & Wed-Fri, to 9pm Tue, 11am-5pm Sat & Sun; 🚌 14 from Rådhuspladsen to the nearest stop, Tuborg Blvd; &

This frenetic, dizzying museum is dedicated to inspiring children's interest in nature, technology, the environment and health. This is a genuinely exciting, hands-on experience and kids adore it. As well as all the permanent experiments there is a changing program of temporary themed exhibitions – previous ones have included dinosaurs, robots and Sports & Spinach. This 4100 sq m museum opened in 1991 and is located a little north of the city centre, along the coast, in the old brewery harbour beside the poshest suburb in the city. There is a cafe and shop on-site.

WORTH THE TRIP

Louisiana Museum of Modern Art (☎ 49 19 07 19; www.louisiana.dk; Gammel Strandvej 13, Humlebæk; adult/child under 18yr 95kr/free; ◷ 11am-11pm Tue-Fri, to 6pm Sat & Sun; 🚌 Humlebæk) is one of the finest modern art museums in Scandinavia. As well as world-class art from the constructivist, pop art, nouveau realist and other movements, the museum also has an elegant concert hall with regular Friday classical concerts, a cafe with outdoor seating alongside lawns that stretch down to the sea and a vibrant children's section. Along with the permanent collection, the museum also offers six to eight temporary exhibitions each year – check the website for details. These temporary exhibitions draw huge crowds, particularly at weekends. The original manor house, dating from 1855, has been extended over the years and is situated on the outskirts of the affluent coastal town of Humlebæk, 35km north of Copenhagen. It is 36 minutes by train from Central Station and another 10 minutes on foot to the museum (there are signposts – you turn left once you reach the main road in front of Humlebæk station). See also p14.

All hands on hard hats at the Experimentarium

SHOP

The main shopping streets in Nørrebro are Nørrebrogade itself, a busy, local shopping street; Blågårdsgade, just off it to the west, which has a couple of nice cafes and fashion stores; and Elmegade, the trendy heart of the area – indeed of the city – where some of the hippest clothing stores rub shoulders with sushi and bagel places. Nearby Ravnsborggade is the best place in the city for vintage jewellery, kitschy furniture and antiques – although the bric-a-brac and antique shops are increasingly being pushed out by new men's and women's fashion stores these days.

Østerbrogade is Østerbro's main shopping street, with Nødre Frihavnsgade another good bet. Apart perhaps from Normann (p107) there aren't really any shops that make a visit to Østerbro worthwhile in themselves, but there is a good mix of midrange shops here if you feel like a change from Strøget and its environs.

FÆLLEDPARKEN
🚌 1A, 15, 42, 43, 150S; ♿
Copenhagen's largest park is a functional, if not especially attractive, open space popular with amateur footballers. It is dominated by the giant concrete monolith of Parken (p115), the national stadium.

ZOOLOGISK MUSEUM
☎ 35 32 10 01; www.zoologi.snm.ku.dk; Universitetsparken 15, Østerbro; adult/child 75/40kr; 🕙 10am-5pm Tue-Sun; 🚌 18, 42, 43, 150S, 184, 185; ♿
With its interesting display of stuffed animals, sealife and birds, Copenhagen's zoological museum is popular with kids.

ANTIKHALLEN *Antiques*
☎ 35 35 04 20; Sortedams Dossering 7C, Nørrebro; 🕙 2-6pm Mon-Fri, 11am-3pm Sat; 🚌 5A, 350S
One of the best antique furniture and bric-a-brac shops in this excellent antique area, with a wide range of styles and periods.

☐ FREDERIKSEN *Fashion*

☎ 35 35 05 66; Ravnsborggade 15, Nørrebro; ☺ 11am-6pm Tue-Fri, 11am-3pm Sat; 🚌 3A, 5A, 350S

Lise Frederiksen's super-feminine clothing boutique is just one of several new fashion shops on what used to be thought of as the city's top antiques street. Her store is joined by Dico, Stig P, Riktigt and the groovy gift shop Kiertner (all are located on Ravnsborggade) in the ongoing trendification of this area.

☐ FROGEYE *Footwear*

☎ 35 37 01 39; Blågårdsgade 2a, Nørrebro; ☺ 10am-6pm Mon-Thu, to 7pm Fri, to 4pm Sat; 🚌 3A, 5A, 350S

This is one of the grooviest shoe shops in the city. It has a wide range of Camper footwear always in stock.

☐ FÜNF *Fashion*

☎ 33 37 13 80; www.funf.dk; Elmegade 2, Nørrebro; ☺ 11am-6pm Mon-Fri, to 3pm Sat; 🚌 3A, 5A, 350S,

This gorgeous women's clothing store on trendy Elmegade stocks up-to-the-second ranges from several local designers.

Discover the art of good coffee at the Coffee Collective (p111)

NEIGHBOURHOODS

NØRREBRO & ØSTERBRO

WORTH THE TRIP

Dyrehaven (Klampenborg; 🚆 S-train Klampenborg; ♿) is a 1000-hectare former royal hunting ground much loved by joggers, cyclists, rollerbladers and picnickers (it is also the best place to bring a toboggan when there's snow). You can drive – though there is not much parking – via the coast road to Klampenborg. The turning for the park entrance is on the left (if you are coming from the city) just after Bellevue Beach (on your right) and Arne Jacobsen's celebrated Bellevue theatre and apartment complex (on your left). But it is quicker by train – just 22 minutes from Central Station. Klampenborg Station is right beside the main gate to the park.

Dyrehaven is also home to the 1538-founded **Bakken** (☎ 39 63 35 44; www.bakken .dk; Dyrehavevej 62, Klampenborg; admission free, multiride wristband 219kr weekends, holidays & end Jun–mid-Aug, 199kr all other times; 🕙 daily end Mar–late Aug; 🚆 S-train Klampenborg, then 800m walk), which is said to be the world's oldest amusement park. The cynical might say it looks it, but if you approach it in the right frame of mind (admittedly, a couple of beers and some candy floss helps), Bakken can be a lot of fun. This is very much an old-school funfair experience, with creaking 1970s rides, tame rollercoasters, appalling fast food and cheesy cabarets. There are about 33 rides in all, as well as roughly 40 cafes and restaurants. See website for specific opening times.

There are several of these slightly edgy fashion boutiques nearby, including Goggle, Resteröds, Bark, Cappalis and, just around the corner on Guldbergsgade, Weiz.

📷 **NORMANN**
Homeware/Furniture/Fashion
☎ 35 55 44 59; www.normann
-copenhagen.com; Østerbrogade 70,
Østerbro; 🕙 10am-6pm Mon-Fri, to 4pm
Sat; 🚌 1A, 14, 15; ♿
This recently opened, 1700-sq-metre clothing and interior design store is housed in a vast, white-washed vault – formerly a cinema – on Østerbro's main shopping street. As well as stocking its own award-winning brand of home-wares (including the famous rubber

washing-up bowls, collapsible 'Funnel' strainer, stemless cognac glasses and outlandish cardboard lampshades), Normann also stocks vintage-style sportswear, furniture and Alessi homewares, and clothing by Joseph and Resteröds. Think of it as a more cutting-edge Illums Bolighus (p62).

📷 **VELOUR** *Fashion*
☎ 35 35 60 64; www.velour.se;
Elmegade 21; 🕙 11am-6pm Mon-Fri,
11am-3.30pm Sat; 🚌 3A, 5A, 350S
Flying the flag for Gothenburg fashion, unisex Velour is a sound choice for getting that Swedish preppy look, with everything from skinny ties to pastel pants. Next door, Resteröds (same opening

hours) peddles an edgier Scandi look, with street-smart printed tees and chequered indie-hipster shirts.

🍴 EAT

🍴 BODEGA *Global* €€

☎ 35 39 07 07; www.bodega.dk; Kapelvej 1, Nørrebro; ⏰ 10am-midnight Mon-Thu, to 3am Fri & Sat, to 9pm Sun; 🚌 5A, 350S

This recently renamed and re-invigorated DJ bar-cafe-restaurant beside the walls of Assistens Kirkegård (p104) is one of the hot spots in this hottest of neighbourhoods. The fresh-thinking fusion kitchen is accomplished and soul, funk and R&B grooves are spun on Friday and Saturday nights.

🍴 CAFÉ Ñ *Vegetarian* €

☎ 35 35 11 62; Blågårdsgade 17, Nørrebro; ⏰ 8am-10pm Sat-Thu, to midnight Fri; 🚌 3A, 5A, 350S

Options at this vegetarian cafe include salubrious soups, veggie burgers, smoothies and juices. From 6pm on Fridays, the week's special dish is a bargain 25kr. Get in early! Kitchen closes 9pm.

🍴 DAG H *Franco-Danish* €€

☎ 35 27 63 00; www.dagh.dk; Dag Hammarskjölds Allé 36-40; ⏰ 8am-9.30pm Mon-Fri, 10am-9.30pm Sat, 10am-9pm Sun; 🚌 1A, 14, 15; ♿

Formerly the coffee temple Amokka, Dag H now takes the name of the street on which it stands and remains the prime weekend brunch destination (when it is best to book in advance) for the locally resident young professionals with kids in tow. One of the city's larger cafes, it boasts a beautiful, contemporary interior and plenty of outdoor seating in summer with a short but predictable menu of French brasserie classics, burg-

---

WORTH THE TRIP

Architect Zaha Hadid's sexy, slinky glass and stone extension put **Ordrupgaard** (☎ 39 64 11 83; www.ordrupgaard.dk; Vilvordevej 110, Charlottenlund; adult/under 12yr 85kr/free; ⏰ 1-5pm Tue & Thu & Fri, 1pm-7pm Wed, 11am-5pm Sat & Sun; 🚉 S-train Klampenborg, then 🚌 388; ♿) on the international map when it opened in 2005. However, this charming art museum, housed in an early-20th-century manor house to the north of Copenhagen, has always had an enviable collection of 19th- and 20th-century art. Works include paintings by Gauguin (who lived in Copenhagen for many years), Renoir and Matisse, as well as notable Danes such as JT Lundbye and Vilhelm Hammershøj. The museum also incorporates the former home of pioneering 20th-century Danish designer Finn Juhl. There is a nice cafe here, too, with outdoor seating in summer.

A stunning fusion of food styles is served at Bodega

ers, fancy sandwiches and salads (their three-course evening menu for 259kr is a good deal). Kontra Coffee next door is the city's best coffee-making equipment store.

🍴 FISCHER *Italian* €€
☎ 35 42 39 64; www.hosfischer.dk; Victor Borges Plads 12; 🕙 11am-midnight Mon-Sat, 10.30am-3pm Sun; 🚌 3A
Set in a converted workers' bar, neighbourly Fischer serves Italian soul food such as freshly made linguini with *aglio e olio* (pasta with garlic, olive oil and chilli). That it's all seriously good isn't surprising considering owner and head chef

David Fischer worked the kitchen at Rome's Michelin-starred La Pergola.

🍴 FRU HEIBERG
Franco-Danish €€€
☎ 35 38 91 00; Rosenvængets Allé 3, Østerbro; 🕙 5-10pm Tue-Thu & Sun, to 11pm Fri & Sat; 🚌 1A, 14, 15
What used to be an old-fashioned Greek restaurant is now one of the most popular restaurants in Østerbro, serving contemporary Franco-Danish food and run by the people behind Gefärlich (p113). It is a lovely, cosy place invariably packed to the rafters with young diners and drinkers

at the weekends, when booking is advised.

🍴 KAFFESALONEN
Franco-Danish €€

☎ 35 35 12 19; Pebling Dossering 6, Nørrebro; ⏱ 8am-midnight Mon-Fri, 10am-midnight Sat & Sun; 🚌 5A, 350S

This lovely cafe-restaurant is right beside the city lakes. Actually, make that *on* the city lakes – during summer it moves out to a floating deck. Perfect for a sundowner.

🍴 KIIN KIIN *Thai* €€€

☎ 35 35 75 55; www.kiin.dk; Guldbergsgade 21; ⏱ 5.30-9pm Mon-Sat; 🚌 3A, 5A, 350S

It ain't cheap, but this Michelin-starred winner does obscenely good things to Thai food (think baby lobster with frozen galangal and tamarind). Book ahead.

🍴 LYST CAFÉ *Cafe* €

☎ 82 30 03 39; Jægersborggade 56, Nørrebro; ⏱ 7.30am-11pm Mon-Thu, to 1am Fri, 10am-1am Sat, 10am-11pm Sun; 🚌 5A, 18, 66, 350S

Head to this kooky and kitsch spot (note the blowfish lamp) for freshly made wraps and perfect *kanelsnegle* (cinnamon rolls).

🍴 NUMÉRO 64
Franco-Danish €€€

☎ 35 35 39 00; www.cofoco.dk; Østerbrogade 64; ⏱ 6-9.30pm Mon-Sat; 🚌 1A, 14, 15

This sexy basement restaurant, with its raw-brick- and glass-walled interior, is run by the Cofoco group (p130). The seasonal set menu offers polished new-Nordic dishes such as fresh goat's cheese with pickled beetroot, crispy rye bread and horseradish, or glazed pork cheeks with Jerusalem artichoke cream, pickled pearl onions, Granny Smith apples and parsley. Inspired flavours; petite servings.

🍴 PUSSY GALORE'S FLYING CIRCUS *Global* €€

☎ 35 37 68 00; www.pussy-galore.dk; Sankt Hans Torv 30, Nørrebro; ⏱ 8am-11pm Sun-Thu, 9am-11pm Fri & Sat; 🚌 3A, 5A, 350S; ♿

This Sankt Hans Torv pioneer remains popular, thanks to a great location on the quarter's most buzzing square, with plenty of outdoor tables and a clever, good-value fusion menu.

🍸 DRINK

If you are looking for bars and clubs catering to a relaxed, predominantly 20- and early-30-something crowd, make a beeline for Nørrebro.

🍸 CAFÉ BOPA *DJ Bar*

☎ 35 43 05 66; www.cafebopa.dk; Løgstørgade 8, Østerbro; ⏱ 9am-midnight Mon-Wed, to 2am Thu, to 5am Fri, 10am-

There's always something brewing at Nørrebro Bryghus (p182)

5am Sat, to midnight Sun; 🚆 **S-train Nordhavn;** 🚌 **1A, 14**
This quiet square in the heart of a residential part of the city throbs to DJ-spun beats at the weekend as Bopa pumps up the volume and transforms into one of the city's best flirty venues.

🍸 COFFEE COLLECTIVE *Cafe*
☎ 60 15 15 25; www.coffeecollective .dk; Jægersborggade 10, Nørrebro; 🕗 7.30am-8pm Mon-Fri, 9am-6pm Sat, 10am-6pm Sun; 🚌 5A, 18, 66, 350S
Situated on up-and-coming Jægersborggade, the tiny Coffee Collective cafe will satisfy the toughest of coffee snobs with its passionate baristi, on-site roasting and fruity espresso.

🍸 HARBO BAR *Bar*
Blågårdsgade 2D 🕗 **8.30am-midnight Mon-Thu, 8.30am-2am Fri, 9.30am-2am Sat, 9.30am-11pm Sun;** 🚌 **3A, 5A, 350S**
Recycled interiors, cheap drinks and the odd exhibition or performance make this lo-fi bar the new hot spot for Nørrebro's cool creatives.

NEIGHBOURHOODS

NØRREBRO & ØSTERBRO

🍸 LAUNDROMAT CAFÉ *Cafe*

☎ 35 35 26 72; Elmegade 15, Nørrebro; 🕑 8am-midnight Sun-Thu, to 2am Fri, 10am-2am Sat; 🚌 3A, 5A, 350S

This playful corner cafe was the brainchild of Icelander Fridrik Weisshappel who decided to turn the old Morgans juice bar into a cafe-laundrette, with washing machines just round the corner from the bar (wonder where he got that idea from?). Throw in 4000 secondhand books (all available to purchase) to decorate the bar and you have one of Copenhagen's most distinctive and enjoyable venues.

🍸 NØRREBRO BRYGHUS *Brewery*

☎ 35 30 05 30; www.noerrebrobryghus .dk; Ryesgade 3, Nørrebro; 🕑 11am-midnight Mon-Thu, to 2am Fri & Sat; 🚌 3A, 5A, 350S

This two-storey brewery with a lounge bar and a good midrange

Do your washing, read a book or just catch up with friends at the Laundromat Café

WORTH THE TRIP

Said to be one of the finest Renaissance palaces in Northern Europe, **Frederiksborg Slot** (☎ 48 26 04 39; www.frederiksborgslot.dk; Hillerød; 🕑 11am-3pm Nov-Mar, 10am-5pm Apr-Oct; adult/concession/child 60/50/15kr; 🚊 S-train Hillerød, 40 min north of Copenhagen, then 10-min walk through town centre; 🚻) was bought by Frederik II in 1560 from a local nobleman. By rights, 'Christiansborg' Slot would be a better name, as Christian IV was both born here in 1577 and built the castle that stands today in its red-brick and sandstone splendour in the Dutch Renaissance style. Following a devastating fire in 1859, the castle was rebuilt using funds from the Carlsberg Foundation and opened as the Museum of National History in 1877, filled with a priceless collection of furniture and art.

restaurant (think crab and mussel salad with radish salad and New York lager-flavoured vinaigrette) kick-started the microbrewing craze a few years back. Thankfully, the concept remains as fresh and alluring as ever.

🍸 OAK ROOM *Bar*
☎ 38 60 38 60; Birkegade 10, Nørrebro; 🕑 8pm-1am Tue & Wed, to 2am Thu, 4pm-4am Fri, 6pm-4am Sat; 🚌 3A, 5A, 350S

If we had to nominate one place to go for a memorable, flirty, drunken Copenhagen evening right now, it would have to be the Oak Room. This sweaty, minimalist, invariably packed two-room cocktail bar is close to trendy Elmegade and just around the corner from Rust (p115).

🍸 TEA TIME *Tearoom*
☎ 35 35 50 58; www.tea-time.dk; Birkegade 3, Nørrebro; 🕑 2-6pm Tue-Thu, 10am-6pm Fri & Sat, noon-6pm Sun; 🚌 3A, 5A, 350S

An improbable but welcome addition to Nørrebro's edgy, underground scene is this super-cute English tearoom. Nibble daintily on homemade cupcakes, pink lemonade, fine teas and finger sandwiches, all served with just a hint of postmodern irony. Cosy and ever-so-slightly camp, it's the kind of place that makes your day better.

⭐ PLAY

🎴 GEFÄRLICH *Club*
☎ 35 24 13 24; Fælledvej 7, Nørrebro; 🕑 11am-midnight Tue, to 2am Wed, to 3am Thu, to 3.30am Fri, 10am-3.30am Sat; 🚌 1A, 14

This deeply groovy bar, club, restaurant, lounge, cafe, hairdresser, art and poetry space (really) has made a major splash on the Nørrebro nightlife scene. It gets packed at weekends, with the

Stephan Sander
Web Designer

Favourite place to meet friends for a drink Gefärlich (p109) on Fælledvej is a nice place to sit outside with a drink on a summer's day, listening to classic jazz. Either there or the Laundromat Café (p112) on Elmegade – a very cosy, crowded and entertaining place. Very Norrebro. **Favourite lunch spot** The cafe at the top of the Post and Tele Museum (p66). The rooftop terrace is spectacular. **Venue for a birthday celebration** Famo (p113) on Saxogade in Vesterbro. Excellent value for money and a relaxed, friendly atmosphere, plus great food. **Copenhagen's 'secret treasure'** The heart of Nørrebro has a lot to offer – everything from modern antiques to reasonably priced meals and funky clothes. **If you're here for a short stop, make the effort to see** The Harbour – it's what makes Copenhagen special.

Entertainment on a grand scale at Parken

incriminating evidence usually posted on its My Space page by midweek.

 PARKEN *Sports/Live Music*
www.parken.dk ; Fælledparken, Øster-bro; 🚌 1A, 14D
Denmark's 22,000-seat (40,000 for concerts) national stadium hosts the city's top football team FCK, major sporting events and visiting rock and pop gods such as U2 and Robbie Williams.

 RUST *Club*
☎ 35 24 52 00; www.rust.dk; Guld-bergsgade 8, Nørrebro; admission varies; 🕑 9pm-5am Wed-Sat; 🚌 3A, 5A, 350S; ♿
Rust is the edgiest of Copenhagen's major clubs. Spaces range from nightclub to live-music hall and lounge, with an equally diverse musical policy. From 11pm, entrance is available only to over 18s (Wednesday and Thursday) and over 20s (Friday and Saturday).

>NØRREPORT TO ØSTERPORT

Denmark is one of the few countries in the world where that hoary old travel-writing cliché 'land of contrasts' doesn't really apply. But this part of its capital, at least, has plenty of wildly different things to offer. On the one hand you have some of Copenhagen's flagship sights as well as the unexpected delights of the Hirschsprungske and Davids Samlingerne (collections). On the other hand, in the area centred on Nansensgade, you have a quietly hip quarter with intriguing boutiques, cool restaurants and laid-back bars.

The area is bordered to the north by the shallow city lakes, originally dug as a fire defence, and to the south by Voldgade, which becomes Øster Voldgade at the junction with Gothersgade. A small geographical liberty has been taken with a detour south (Nørreport really stops at Gothersgade, but it makes sense for the purposes of this guide) to take in Kongens Have and Rosenborg.

NØRREPORT TO ØSTERPORT

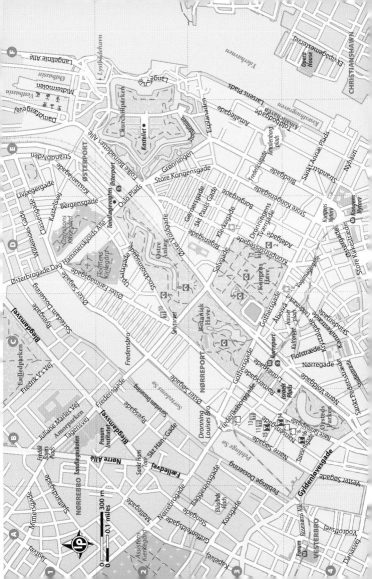

SEE

BOTANISK HAVE

☎ 35 32 22 40; www.botanik.snm
.ku.dk; Gothersgade 128; admission free;
⏱ gardens 8.30am-6pm daily May-Sep,
to 4pm Tue-Sun Oct-Apr, palm house
10am-3pm daily May-Sep, closed Mon
Oct-Apr; Ⓜ Nørreport Ⓡ S-train Nørreport 🚌 6A, 150S, 184, 185, 173E
The beautiful Palmehus (Palm
House) is the main attraction of
this small but appealing botanic
garden with 20,000 species of
plants from around the world. A
Botanic Museum (Gothersgade 130; admission free; ⏱ varies) features exhibits of
plants from Denmark, Greenland
and the rest of the world. There
are two entrances to the garden:
one at the intersection of Gothersgade and Øster Voldgade, and the
other off Øster Farimagsgade.

DAVIDS SAMLING

☎ 33 73 49 49; www.davidmus.dk;
Kronprinsessegade 30; admission free;
⏱ 1-5pm Tue & Fri-Sun, 10am-5pm Wed
& Thu; 🚌 11, 26, 350S
This jewel of a museum houses
Scandinavia's largest collection
of Islamic art, including jewellery,
ceramics and silk, and exquisite
works such as an Egyptian rock
crystal jug from AD 1000 and a
500-year-old Indian dagger inlaid
with rubies. That's all up on the 4th
floor. On your way up, you can also
spend a fruitful couple of hours taking in the museum's fine Danish,
English and French furniture and
art from the 18th and 19th centuries. All of this was bequeathed
to the museum by the barrister
Christian Ludvig David, who died
in 1960, and is maintained by his
foundation. The museum is housed
in his former home, a neoclassical
mansion dating from 1806.

DEN HIRSCHSPRUNGSKE SAMLING

☎ 35 42 03 36; www.hirschsprung.dk;
Stockholmsgade 20; adult/child/conces-

GARDEN STATE

This is not the most obviously picturesque place to wander – Nørre Voldgade and Øster
Voldgade are big, wide, traffic-filled streets – but you can avoid them completely and walk
almost the entire length of this part of the city through the beautifully landscaped gardens
of Ørsteds Parken, Botanisk Have (Botanical Garden) and Østre Anlæg, the landscaped park
behind Statens Museum for Kunst. In the summer months these parks throng with people
enjoying picnics, reading in the sun or, in the case of Ørsteds Parken, a good number of gay
men on the prowl. But the most popular of all is probably Kongens Have (Kings Park), to the
south of Rosenborg, with its formal flower beds, children's puppet theatre and cafe.

Enjoying the Copenhagen summer in Kongens Have

sion 50/free/40kr Thu-Mon, Wed free;
⏰ 11am-4pm Wed-Mon; 🚌 6A, 14, 40,
42, 43; ♿

Giving Davids Samling a run for its money as the city's most under-rated museum is tobacco magnate Heinrich Hirschsprung's collection of Danish art, most of it from the first half of the 19th century, and featuring some of the nation's most treasured paintings from its so-called Golden Age (see p166). The museum displays moving and powerful works by the widely celebrated Funen and Skågen schools, famous for their haunting landscapes and depictions of 'ordinary' Danes and including artists such as Christen Købke, CW Eckersberg and PS Krøyer.

🟢 KONGENS HAVE

Ⓜ Nørreport 🚆 S-train Nørreport
🚌 6A, 184, 185, 350S; ♿

The oldest park in Copenhagen was laid out in the early 17th century by Christian IV, who used it as his vege-table patch. These days it has rather more to offer, including beautiful flower beds, an excellent children's play area and a marionette theatre with free performances during the summer holiday (2pm and 3pm, Tuesday to Sunday).

☉ ROSENBORG SLOT

☎ 33 15 32 86; www.rosenborgslot.dk; Øster Voldgade 4A; adult/child 75kr/free, combined ticket incl Amalienborg Slot 100kr; ☷ vary; Ⓜ Nørreport ⓡ S-train Nørreport ⓑ 6A, 11, 184, 185, 150S, 350S

Copenhagen's stunning Renaissance Palace dates from the early 1600s. Its historic rooms, some of them decorative treasures in their own right, are full of artefacts and art from the royal collection. The crown jewels are in the basement. The carp in the moat are said to have descended from Christian IV's pets/occasional dinner. See also p15. For opening hours, see the website.

☉ STATENS MUSEUM FOR KUNST

☎ 33 74 84 84; www.smk.dk; Sølvgade 48; admission free; ☷ 10am-5pm Tue & Thu-Sun, Wed to 8pm; Ⓜ Nørreport ⓡ S-train Nørreport ⓑ 6A, 26, 150S, 173E, 184, 185; ♿

Denmark's impressive National Gallery (see p22).

🛍 SHOP

This isn't a major shopping area but there are some cool designer boutiques on Nansensgade selling unique fashion clothing, accessories, retro homewares, gifts and 20th-century collectables, and Frederiksborggade has a couple

A new Golden Age for the Copenhagen visual arts? Decide for yourself at the Statens Museum for Kunst

WHEN IN ROME

If you want to blend in with the locals, follow our essential 10-point plan:

> Smoke like a kipper
> Men – throw away your ties
> Women – throw away your bras
> Everyone – get on your bikes
> Throw away that extraneous top layer of bread; have smørrebrød for lunch (see p17)
> Wait for the green man before crossing
> Laugh at the Swedes
> Never serve salmon on brown bread
> Spend big on lampshades
> Don't queue for the bus – it's everyone for themselves!

of outdoor pursuit stores (Spejder Sports at No 32; Fjeld & Fritid at No 28) catering to the climbing, walking and camping crowd.

☐ FRK. LILLA *Fashion*

☎ 24 78 01 85; www.frklilla.dk; Frederiksborggade 41; ⏱ 11am-6pm Mon-Fri, to 3pm Sat; Ⓜ Nørreport Ⓡ S-train Nørreport ⬛ 5A, 350S

Raid the racks at this luxe second-hander, famed for its preloved designer labels. Bag anything from Malene Birger cocktail frocks to Miu Miu heels and Marc Jabobs shades, often at 50% off, and never more than two seasons old.

☐ KENDT *Fashion*

☎ 20 96 29 02; www.kendt.nu; Nansensgade 42; ⏱ noon-6pm Thu & Fri, 10am-2pm Sat; Ⓜ Nørreport Ⓡ S-train Nørreport ⬛ 5A, 11, 14, 40, 42, 43, 350S

Designer Kendt has lured every-one from Danish fashionistas to

American hotel heiresses with his light, girly, vivid cocktail frocks (think chiffon and silk) and more casual threads. Not cheap, but these are limited runs, darling.

☐ LAST BAG *Bags*

☎ 32 11 73 90; http://pietbreinholm .dk; Nansensgade 48; ⏱ 10am-7pm Fri, also by appointment; ⬛ 5A, 11, 14, 40, 42, 43, 350S

This shop has been selling the same design of leather satchel – in large and small and a variety of colours (red, black, white, light brown and dark brown) – since 1954. If you love timeless designs, this is one.

🍴 EAT

🍴 AAMANNS TAKEAWAY

Danish €

☎ 35 55 33 44; Øster Farimagsgade 10; ⏱ smørrebrød 10am-4pm, dinner 5-8pm; ⬛ 14, 40

Clued-up foodies get their smør-rebrød fix at Aamanns, where open sandwiches are seasonal, fresh and contemporary. Variations include a scrumptious beef tartar smørrebrød topped with egg emulsion, tarragon, gherkins, capers, onions and mini-potato chips. Eat in or gobble it up in the neighbouring parks.

🍴 KALASET *Bar-Restaurant* €

☎ 33 33 00 35; www.kalaset.dk; **Vendersgade 16;** ⏱ **11am-midnight Mon-Thu, 10-2am Fri & Sat, 10am-11pm Sun;** 🚌 **5A, 11, 14, 40, 42, 43, 350S**
Under the current owners, this grungy-chic cellar cafe-restaurant on the corner of Nansensgade and Vendersgade is very popular with younger locals.

🍴 ORANGERIET *Danish* €€€

☎ 33 11 13 07; Kronprinsessegade 13; ⏱ **11.30am-3pm & 6-10pm Tue-Sat, 11.30am-3pm Sun;** 🚌 **11, 26, 350S**
Enchantingly set in a vintage orangery in Kongens Have (p119), Orangeriet is one of Copenhagen's newest dining darlings. At the helm is award-winning chef Jasper Kure, whose mod-twist Scandi creations focus on simple flavours and top-notch seasonal produce. Savour the brilliance in dishes such as fried cockerel with thyme, grilled charlotte onions, creamy cauliflower, peas and smoked lard,

> **MIND YOUR MANNERS**
> In Danish there is no direct equivalent for the word 'please'. A polite request is instead expressed by a tone of voice and/or beginning a sentence with phrases such as 'May I...' *(Må jeg...)* or 'Could I...' *(Kunne jeg...).*

or rhubarb trifle with macaroons, cherry liqueur, vanilla and yoghurt sorbet. Knowledgeable staff, an al fresco summertime terrace, and good-value set menus (three courses for 335kr) make this a must for midrange gourmands and true romantics.

🍴 STICKS 'N' SUSHI *Japanese* €€

☎ 33 16 14 07; www.sushi.dk; Nansens-gade 47; ⏱ **11.30am-9.30pm Mon-Wed, 11.30am-10pm Thu-Sat; 2-9.30pm;** 🚌 **5A, 14, 40, 42, 43, 350S;** ♿
The original and still the most stylish contemporary sushi place in Copenhagen, with especially good tuna tartare and hamachi carpaccio options. Other branches crop up in various areas of the city, including Vesterbro – check online for a comprehensive listing of locations.

🍸 DRINK
🍸 BANKERÅT *Bar*

☎ 33 93 69 88; www.bankeraat.dk; Ahlefeldtsgade 27-29; ⏱ 9.30am-

Rune RK
DJ, music producer and mind behind dance hit 'Calabria'

Calabria was inspired by… A gig I played in Calabria. My records were stolen, there were mobsters and the organisers wouldn't pay up. **Top electronic music festivals in town…** Include Raw (www.rawcph.com) and the ever-crazy Copenhagen Distortion (p26), a collection of street parties around the city playing some pop and lots of underground electronica. Strøm (www.stromcph .dk) is more civilised and family-friendly. **Danish electronic music…** Has exploded with talent such as Lulu Rouge, Noir, Lasbas and Kjeld Tolstrup. Andres Trentemøller has strongly influenced the local sound, which is melancholic and atmospheric but danceable. **To experience the local scene…** Scan www.hifly .dk. Culture Box (p125) is a safe bet for Danish electronica, especially if the locals are playing. Simons (p91) is the new hot spot. Rust (p115) is more commercial but still fun, and Zoo Bar (p69) is a good preclubbing weekend hang-out. For jazz, don't miss La Fontaine (p71).

midnight Mon-Fri, 10.30am-midnight Sat-Sun; 🚌 11, 14, 40, 42, 43
This characterful, cultish cafe-bar has been part of the Nansensgade scene since before there even was a scene. Check out porn-adorned loos and freaky taxidermy by local artist Phillip Jensen.

🍷 BIBENDUM *Wine Bar*
☎ 33 33 07 74; www.vincafeen.dk; Nansensgade 45; 🕐 4pm-midnight Mon-Sat; Ⓜ Nørreport 🚆 S-train Nørreport 🚌 11, 14, 40, 42, 43

Copenhagen's best wine bar is situated in a cosy, rustic cellar on trendy Nansensgade and serves more than 30 wines – from Australia, New Zealand, Spain, France, Italy and Austria – by the glass. Intimate but relaxed, and blessedly free of wine snobs, although the bar staff are extremely knowledgeable.

🍷 OLD MATE *Cafe*
☎ 50 45 47 23; Nansensgade 26; 🕐 8.30am-6pm Tue-Fri, noon-6pm

Surround yourself with characterful decor in Nørreport's perennial drinking hole, Bankeråt (p122)

NEIGHBOURHOODS

NØRREPORT TO ØSTERPORT

Sat; Ⓜ **Nørreport** Ⓡ **S-train Nørreport** 🚌 **5A, 14, 40, 42, 43, 66, 350S**
Killer coffee, indie-hip regulars and diversions such as dominoes spell lo-fi cool. Snack on Coco Pops or plug into the free wi-fi.

⭐ PLAY
🎭 CULTURE BOX *Club*
☎ 33 32 50 50; www.culture-box.com; **Kronprinsessegade 54; club admission 70kr;** 🕑 **bar 8pm-late Fri & Sat, club usually midnight-6am Fri & Sat;** 🚌 **11, 26**
If you're after a serious dance-floor session, don't miss this iconic Copenhagen club. Spread over two levels, Culture Box ditches cheesy commercial hits for innovative, noncommercial beats spanning anything (and everything) from electro, techno and house to drum'n'bass, dub-step and electronic jazz. Local talent aside, guest DJs have included Cologne's Tobias Thomas and Chicago's Billy Dalessandro. Next door you'll find **Cocktail Box**, handy for a preclub swill.

🎬 FILMHUSETS CINEMATEK
Cinema
☎ 33 74 34 12, restaurant 33 74 34 17; www.dfi.dk; Gothersgade 55; 🕑 9.30am-10pm Tue-Fri, noon-10pm Sat & Sun, closed Jul; 🚌 11, 350S; ♿
The Danish Film Institute's cutting-edge film centre plays classic Danish and foreign film, mostly in short, themed seasons. There is an excellent **cinema bookshop** (🕑 noon-6pm Tue-Sun, closed Jul) here, as well as the stylish restaurant **Sult**.

>VESTERBRO & FREDERIKSBERG

Vesterbro was once a working-class area known for its butchers and prostitutes. In the late 1990s its proximity to the city centre began to draw in the artsy crowd, followed by the young professionals and, predictably, housing prices skyrocketed. Now it has some of the city's coolest restaurants, cafes, shops and nightlife. It fans out in a westerly direction from the city's Central Station.

Leafy, stately Frederiksberg begins further west at Frederiksberg Allé. This broad, tree-lined avenue is lined with *fin de siècle* apartment blocks – some of the most desirable in the city. It finishes at Frederiksberg Have (p128), the city's most romantic park, with a boating lake, rolling lawns and, looking down from the hill, Frederiksborg Slot and Copenhagen Zoo (p129). Ten minutes or so south of here – in Valby – is the world-famous Carlsberg Brewery (p128) with its free museum and visitors centre.

VESTERBRO & FREDRIKSBERG

SEE

CARLSBERG VISITOR CENTRE

☎ 33 27 12 82; www.visitcarlsberg.dk; Gamle Carlsberg Vej 11, Valby; adult/child under 12 yr/12-17 yr 65/free/50kr; 🕙 10am-5pm Tue-Sun year-round, to 7.30pm Thu May-Aug; 🚌 18, 26; ♿

Carlsberg is one of the largest breweries in the world. It was founded by Christian Jacobsen in 1801 but when Christian's son, Jacob, moved it to the borders of Valby and Frederiksberg in 1847 he renamed the brewery after his son Carl (Carlsberg means 'Carl's Hill'). Soon the company was producing over a million bottles a year, and donating millions of kroner to museums and foundations in Denmark. The recently renovated Carlsberg Visitor Centre offers an entertaining journey through the beer-making process and the story of Carlsberg's global success, with a beer or two at the end included in the price.

FREDERIKSBERG HAVE

Main entrance Frederiksberg Runddel; 🚌 18, 26; ♿

This is Copenhagen's most romantic park, with lakes, woodlands and lovely picnic lawns. Overlooking it all is Frederiksborg Slot, a former royal palace, now home to the Royal Danish Military Academy and not generally open to the public.

KØBENHAVNS BYMUSEET

☎ 33 21 07 72; www.copenhagen.dk; Vesterbrogade 59, Vesterbro; adult/concession/child 20/10kr/free; 🕙 10am-5pm, Fri free; 🚌 6A, 26

The city museum is looking a little old-fashioned these days but if you want to find out how Copenhageners used to live, this 18th-century former palace is the place to find out.

Bottled up at the Carlsberg Visitor Centre

URBAN STROLL

Istedgade is one of the most charismatic and surprising streets in Copenhagen. The Central Station end is home to the city's infamous sex industry, with shop window displays that would make a Dutchman blush. The junkies and hookers still linger here but persevere a little further and you will find the numerous quirky shops, cafes and bars that have helped transform Vesterbro into one of the city's hippest quarters in recent years. Take a detour left into Kødbyen, Copenhagen's uberhip 'Meatpacking District', home to brilliant nosh spots **Paté Paté** (p132) and **Kødbyens Fiskebar** (p132), artist-designed bar **Karriere** (p134) and edgy **V1 Gallery** (below).

🄲 NY CARLSBERG VEJ 68

www.nycarlsbergvej68.dk; Ny Carlsberg Vej 68; 🕑 **noon-5pm Tue-Fri, to 3pm Sat during exhibitions;** 🚌 **6A, 10,**

This disused Carlsberg garage, on the outskirts of Vesterbro, is now home to four fascinating art spaces. Top of the heap is **Galleri Nicolai Wallner**, considered a major player on the contemporary Danish art scene (artists represented here include Jeppe Hein and Berlin-based Nordic duo Michael Elmgreen and Ingar Dragset). Neighbouring gallery **Nils Stærk** is equally established and renowned, while newcomer **IMO** mixes cutting-edge art with broader cultural events such as retro film screenings and performances. Next door, **BKS Garage** provides an exhibition platform for current students of the Royal Danish Academy of Fine Arts.

🄲 V1 GALLERY

☎ **33 31 03 21; www.v1gallery.com; Flæsketorvet 69-71, Vesterbro;** 🕑 **noon-6pm Wed-Fri, to 4pm Sat;** 🚌 **10**

V1 Gallery is one of Copenhagen's most progressive art galleries, showcasing fresh work from both emerging and established local and foreign artists. Some of the world's hottest names in street- and graffiti art have exhibited here, from Britain's Banksy to America's Todd James and Lydia Fong (aka Barry McGee).

🄲 ZOOLOGISK HAVE

☎ **72 20 02 00; www.zoo.dk; Roskildevej 32, Frederiksberg; adult/child 120/60kr;** 🕑 **9am-4pm Mon-Fri, to 5pm Sat & Sun Mar, to 5pm Mon-Fri, to 6pm Sat & Sun Apr & May, to 9.30pm Jul & Aug, to 5pm Mon-Fri, to 6pm Sat & Sun Sep, to 5pm Oct, to 4pm Nov-Feb;** 🚌 **6A;** ♿

The giraffe house is a major attraction in the city's impressive zoo, but 2007 saw the opening of a state-of-the-art elephant house designed by British architect Sir Norman Foster.

NEIGHBOURHOODS

VESTERBRO & FREDRIKSBERG

Granola serves delicious cafe treats (p132)

SHOP

As well as being home to Copenhagen's porn industry and an improbable number of cheap men's hairdressers, Istedgade has some of the most interesting fashion boutiques in the city.

DESIGNER ZOO
Homewares

☎ 33 24 94 93; www.dzoo.dk; Vesterbrogade 137, Vesterbro; ⏲ 10am-5.30pm Mon-Thur, to 7pm Fri, to 3pm Sat; 🚌 6A

Denmark's renowned design mojo finds its contemporary home at this supercool interior and fashion complex at the unfashionable end of Vesterbrogade. Here, fashion and furniture designers, as well as ceramic artists and glass blowers, work and sell their highly desirable, limited-edition creations.

EAT

APROPOS
Global €€€

☎ 33 23 12 21; www.cafeapropos.dk; Halmtorvet 12, Vesterbro; ⏲ 10am-midnight Mon-Thu & Sun, to 1am Fri & Sat; 🚆 S-train Central Station 🚌 10; ♿

One of the leading lights of this rejuvenated cafe square, Apropos serves a free-roaming menu that includes lobster rolls, tandoori salmon and New York cheesecake. There's plenty of outdoor seating during summer.

BIO MIO *Global* €€

☎ 33 31 20 00; www.biomio.dk; Halmtorvet 19; ⏲ 5-10pm Mon-Wed, noon-10pm Thu-Sun; 🚌 10

Once a BOSCH store (note the neon sign), this salubrious designer canteen is one of only two 100% organic restaurants in Denmark.

COFOCO *French* €€

☎ 33 13 60 60; www.cofoco.dk; Abel Cathrines Gade 7, Vesterbro; ⏲ 5.30-9.30pm Mon-Sat; 🚌 6A, 10, 26

If Copenhagen Food Consulting merely offered a superb four-course menu, featuring such delights as pork tenderloin with pork cheeks, parsnip and apricots or veal braised in red wine with celery and wild mushrooms, for just 250kr – well, that alone would warrant it a high ranking on the list of the city's best restaurants. But this is a stylish and convivial place too, with diners eating on a giant, communal wooden table beneath sparkling chandeliers. The same owners run the excellent Les Trois Cochons (p132) and Auberge in Østerbro.

Ⅲ DYREHAVEN *Cafe/Bar* €
www.dyrehavenkbh.dk; Sønder Blvd 72, Vesterbro; ⏰ 9am-midnight Mon-Wed, 9am-2am Thu & Fri, 10am-2am Sat, 10am-6pm Sun; 🚌 10

Once a spit-and-sawdust working-class bar (the vinyl booths and easy-wipe floors tell the story), Dyrehaven is now a second home for Vesterbro's cool, young bohemians. Squeeze into your skinny jeans and join them for cheap drinks, simple tasty grub (the 'Kartoffelmad' egg open sandwich is a classic, made with homemade mayo and fried shallots) and chilled late-night camaraderie.

Ⅲ FAMO *Italian* €€
☎ 33 23 22 50; Saxogade 3, Vesterbro; ⏰ 6-10pm; 🚌 6A, 26
This authentic Italian is usually crowded to the gunwales with enthusiastic foodie locals enjoying a

WORTH A TRIP
Arken (☎ 43540222; www.arken.dk; Skovvej 100, Ishøj; adult/child/concession 85/free/70kr; ⏰ 10am-5pm Tue & Thu-Sun, to 9pm Wed) was built to mark Copenhagen's stint as European City of Culture in 1996. This remarkable contemporary art museum is as famed for the building that houses it – its nautical ship-shape inspired by its beachfront location on Ishøj Strand – as the international art contained within. After a few years in the doldrums, Arken has bounced back with a new extension opened in 2008. The permanent collection of works created after 1990 includes stunning pieces by top Danish artists such as Jeppe Hein, Peter Holst and Jacob Kirkegaard. One recent acquisition is Olafur Eliasson's ambitious installation *Your Negotiable Panorama*, which uses visitors' movements to manipulate wavelike light projections. Equally engrossing is Arken's changing program of temporary exhibitions that can focus on photography, art or sculpture. The museum has a book store and a wonderful cafe that hangs, as if it were the ship's lifeboat, on the side of the building – the views across Køge Bay are extraordinary. It is a great place to come with kids as there is plenty of sandy beach space to let off steam after pondering the meaning of Jeff Koon's gigantic flower balloon sculpture. Ishøj Strand is 25 minutes south of Copenhagen. To get to Arden by car, take the E20 motorway and leave at junction 26, following signs for Ishøj Strand. S-trains (lines A or E) leave Copenhagen Central Station twice an hour. From Ishøj station take bus 128, which goes directly to the museum.

DINE WITH THE DANES

If you find yourself travelling to Copenhagen alone, or even with others for that matter, a great way to enjoy some local company is to get in touch with **Dine with the Danes** (www .dinewiththedanes.dk). Originally started by the tourist board in the 1970s, Dine with the Danes restarted as a private operation in 1998 – with some of the original hosts still going strong – offering dinners in the homes of local people. The dinners (adult/child under 8yr/8-15yr 400/free/200kr) consist of two to three courses, coffee and pastries. Fill in the online request form a week or so in advance and the group will do its best to match you up with an appropriate host (there are gay families available, too). More importantly, you'll get to learn more about Denmark and Danish culture straight from the horse's mouth.

fixed menu that might include wild mushroom risotto, squash puree and long-cooked tomato sauces with fresh, homemade pastas.

🍽 GRANOLA *Cafe* €
☎ 40 82 41 20; Værndemsvej 5, Vesterbro; 🕑 7am-6pm Mon-Thu, to 7pm Fri, 9am-5pm Sat, to 4pm Sun; 🚌 6A, 14, 15, 26

An atmospheric mix of industrial lamps, 'General Store' cabinets, and lovingly worn tabletops, Granola serves fresh cafe-grub-like salads, as well as heavenly shakes and juices. Gluttons shouldn't miss the dainty iced muffins or, even better, the sublime ice cream, straight from a small Jutland dairy.

🍽 KØDBYENS FISKEBAR
Seafood €€€
☎ 32 15 56 56; www.fiskebaren.dk; Flæsketorvet 100, Vesterbro; 🕑 6pm-midnight Tue-Thu, to 3am Fri & Sat; 🚌 10

Postindustrial cool (concrete floors, tiled walls and a 1000-litre aquarium) meets sterling

seafood at this Michelin-listed must. In the trendy Meatpacking District, its seasonal menu keeps it simple and fresh with dishes such as Limfjorden blue mussels with steamed apple cider and herbs. There's usually a meat and vegetarian option, and delectable desserts include English liquorice with sea buckthorn and white chocolate ice cream. Kitchen closes 11pm.

🍽 LES TROIS COCHONS
French €€
☎ 33 31 70 55; www.cofoco.dk; Værndemsvej 10, Vesterbro; 🕑 noon-2.30pm & 5.30-10pm Mon-Sat, 5.30-9pm Sun; 🚌 6A, 14, 15, 26

This small but glamorous modern French bistro on the so-called 'food street' heaves with a bubbling mix of diners every night of the week. Its fixed evening menu (starter, main and dessert) for 275kr has to be one of the city's great dining bargains.

🍴 MIELCKE & HURTIGKARL
Modern European €€€

☎ 38 34 84 36; www.mielcke-hurtigkarl
.dk; Frederiksberg Runddel 1, Frederiksberg; 🕙 lunch & dinner Wed-Sun
Apr-Sep, dinner Thu-Sat Oct-Mar, closed
mid-Dec–mid-Jan; 🚌 14, 15 18, 26
If you plan on seducing someone
(or just your own taste buds), book
a table at this culinary charmer. Set
in a former royal summer house
in Frederiksberg Have (p128), its
forest soundscapes, lighting installation and whimsical murals are
utterly dreamy. While the set lunch
menu offers simpler, cheaper fare,
the highlight here is the set dinner
menu, showcasing head chef Jakob
Mielcke's inspired approach to
local and global ingredients (think
Norwegian lobster jelly with salty
plum ice cream).

🍴 PATÉ PATÉ
Modern European €€€

☎ 39 69 55 57; www.patepate.dk;
Slagterboderne 1, Vesterbro; 🕙 8am-
midnight Sun-Wed, to 1am Thu, to 3am
Fri & Sat; 🚌 10
Run by the team behind Falernum
(p134) and Bibendum (p124),
this buzzing restaurant–wine bar
occupies a former pâté factory,
complete with original industrial
fixtures and warm vintage touches.
Here, Euro classics get modern
twists in gems including *poussin*
with liver crostini, pickled cherries

and summer truffle, and perfectly
flaky *tarte fine* with potato, taleg-
gio and rosemary. Hip yet convivial, bonus extras include a clued-up
staff, a well-versed wine list and
close proximity to late-night party
hot spots Bakken (below), Karriere
(p134) and Jolene (p135). Kitchen
closes 11pm. Book ahead.

🍴 SICILIANSK IS *Gelateria* €

☎ 30 22 30 89; www.sicilianskis.dk; Skydebanegade 3, Vesterbro; 🕙 noon-9pm
May-Aug, 1-6pm Apr & Sep; 🚌 10
Honing their skills in Sicily, gelato
meisters Michael and David churn
out the city's best gelato. Go to
town on smooth, seasonal flavours
such as Koldskål (a frozen take on
the classic Danish buttermilk and
lemon dessert).

🍸 DRINK

🍸 BAKKEN *Bar*
Flæsketorvet 19-21, Vesterbro; 🕙 9pm-
4am Thu-Sat; 🚌 10
Affordable drinks, DJ-spun disco
and rock, and a Meatpacking District address make intimate, gritty
Bakken a magnet for attitude-free
hipsters.

🍸 BANG OG JENSEN
Cafe/Bar
🕙 33 25 53 18; www.bangogjensen
.dk; Istedgade 130, Vesterbro; 🕙 8am-
2am Mon-Fri, 10am-2am Sat, 10am-
midnight Sun; 🚌 10

This was one of the pioneers during Vesterbro's regeneration days, bringing a young party crowd to what was then the unfashionable end of Istedgade. Appealingly squashy sofas invite you to waste the afternoon here among the crowd of dudes and DJs in this grungy but adorable venue.

▼ FALERNUM *Wine Bar*
☎ 33 22 30 89; www.falernum.dk; Værnedamsvej 16, Vesterbro; ☾ 8am-midnight Mon-Thu, to 2am Fri, 10am-2am Sat, to midnight Sun; 🚌 6A, 15, 26
Worn floorboards and chairs, bottled-lined shelves and soothing tunes set the scene at this mellow cafe and wine bar. Expect 40 wines by the glass alone, as well as boutique beers, coffee and nosh such as tapas and cheeses.

▼ KAFFE & VINYL *Cafe*
☎ 61 70 33 49; Skydebanegade 4, Vesterbro; ☾ 8am-6pm Mon-Fri, 10am-6pm Sat, 11am-6pm Sun; 🚌 10
Killer caffeine, cultish records and indie-hip regulars define the details at this tiny Vesterbro favourite. Guzzle a velvety latte and bag that Blaxploitation disc.

▼ KARRIERE *Bar*
☎ 33 21 55 09; www.karrierebar.com; Flæsketorvet 57-67, Vesterbro; ☾ 4pm-midnight Thu, to 4am Fri & Sat; 🚌 10

The brainchild of artist Jeppe Hein, this postindustrial bar is another Meatpacking District must, designed by 25 local and international artists: Olafur Eliasson designed the lamps and Jeppe Hein designed the bar, which moves 35mm every 30 minutes. Ditch the so-so food for crafty cocktails, which may include the legendary Mario Mantequilla, made with peanut butter–infused *corralejo blanco* tequila and agave syrup.

▼ RICCO'S COFFEE BAR *Coffee*
☎ 33 31 04 40; www.riccos.dk; Istedgade 119, Vesterbro; ☾ 8am-11pm Mon-Fri, 9am-11pm Sat & Sun; 🚌 10
Vesterbro's groovy locals love this tiny but dedicated coffee bar. Considered by many to be the best coffee bar in Copenhagen, it also sells 20 different types of beans and syrups to take home.

▼ SALON 39 *Cocktail Bar*
☎ 39 20 80 39; www.salon39.dk; Vodroffsvej 39, Frederiksberg; ☾ 4-11.30pm Wed & Thu, to 1.30am Fri & Sat; 🚌 14, 15, 29
An off-the-radar gem, where chandeliers and gilded cornices meet brilliant cocktails (the Penicillin No 39 is dangerously good). Line the stomach with tasty grub including calamari with black-ink mayonnaise.

⭐ PLAY

⭐ DANSESCENEN *Dance*

☎ 33 29 10 10, box office 33 29 10 29; www.dansescenen.dk; Pasteursvej 20, Vesterbro; ⏱ vary; 🚌 6A, 18, 26

Set in a disused mineral-water factory, and close to gallery hub Ny Carlsberg Vej 68 (p129), Dansescenen remains Copenhagen's leading contemporary dance venue. Expect more than 20 international-standard productions each year. Performance times on website.

⭐ DGI-BYEN *Sports*

☎ 33 29 80 00; www.dgi-byen.dk; Tietgensgade 65; 🚆 Central Station 🚌 1A, 65E; ♿

Lying just south of Central Station, overlooking the tracks, you'll find Copenhagen's best leisure and sports complex, featuring a large indoor swimming pool, bowling alley, spa, restaurant, cafe and hotel, among other facilities. On offer at the spa are a wide range of beauty treatments, different massage therapies, algae and salt baths, mud packs and acupuncture.

⭐ FORUM *Live Music*

☎ 32 47 20 00; www.forumcopenhagen. dk; Julius Thomsensplads, Frederiksberg; Ⓜ Forum 🚌 2A; ♿

This is one of the city's major concert venues – Bob Dylan and Metallica have performed here in recent years.

⭐ IMAX TYCHO BRAHE PLANETARIUM *Cinema*

☎ 33 12 12 24; www.tycho.dk; Gammel Kongevej 10, Vesterbro; adult/child 3-12yr 130/80kr; ⏱ 11.30am-8.30pm Mon, 9.30am-8.30pm Tue-Sun; 🚆 S-train Vesterport 🚌 14, 15; ♿

This impressive Imax cinema, named after the famous Danish astronomer, shows fast-paced nature and adventure films on a 1000 sq m screen. It has a domed space theatre that offers a show of the night sky using state-of-the-art equipment.

⭐ JOLENE BAR *Bar/Club*

www.myspace.com/jolenebar; Flæsketorvet 81-85, Vesterbro; ⏱ 5pm-2am Sun-Thu, to 3am Fri & Sat; 🚌 10

Opened by two Icelandic women, this intimate bar and club lines up some serious DJ talent (think Danish techno god Trentemøller), who spin from a circus-themed DJ booth.

⭐ VEGA *Club/Live Music*

☎ 33 25 70 11; www.vega.dk; Enghavevej 40, Vesterbro; 🚌 3A, 10; ♿

Vega is considered the father of all Copenhagen nightlife venues yet, despite its venerable status, it remains both a cutting-edge venue for the most in-demand DJs in Europe, as well as the

You can't beat Vega for top DJs and international music acts

preferred destination of global stars such as Prince, Jamie Cullum and Arctic Monkeys. Store Vega hosts the major live acts. Lilla Vega is a great place to catch the up-and-comers of the music world and becomes the Vega Nightclub and Lounge at weekends. The Ideal Bar allows you to lounge in style with a cocktail in one hand, and plays easy listening grooves as a soundtrack.

>EXCURSIONS

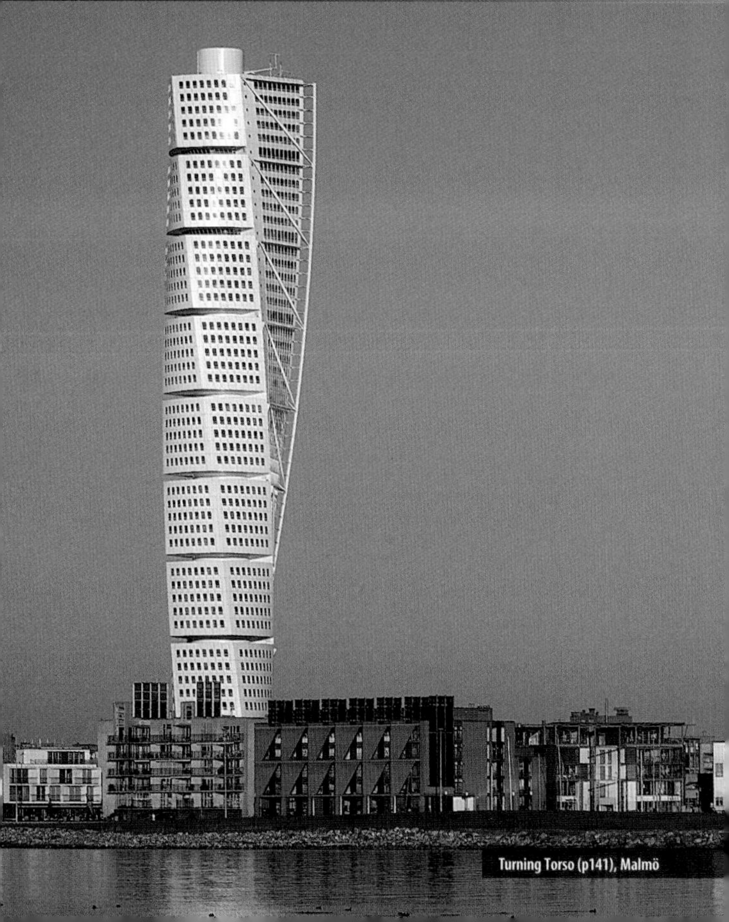

Turning Torso (p141), Malmö

>MALMÖ

If you like Copenhagen, chances are Malmö, the third-largest city in Sweden, will tickle your fancy too. This is a beautiful, lively university city, with a historic centre surrounded by a moat, two grand squares – Stortorget and Gustav Adolfs Torg – and one smaller, cosier cobbled square, Lilla Torg (the mainstream nightlife hotspot with an ice rink in winter). There are wonderful landscaped parks, an excellent art museum, a 15th-century castle filled with yet more museums and a magnificent sandy beach with a traditional cold-bathhouse. In the last five years the city's western harbour has undergone an astonishing transformation into one of the most progressive housing projects in Northern Europe, with the landmark Turning Tower by Spanish architect Santiago Calatrava at its heart.

Until the mid-17th century this part of Sweden was actually Danish territory, so you can think of it as the Danish capital's baby brother (just don't tell the Swedes), but with an even more laid-back vibe and surprisingly buzzing nightlife thanks to a large student population. This is an even smaller city so virtually all the main sights are within easy walking distance. But, a caveat: Malmö is a summer city to a greater extent than Copenhagen; its 290,000 inhabitants hibernate somewhat in the darker months of the year. If you are here for summer, aim for the third week in August, when over 1.6 million people visit the city for the Malmö festival to experience music, theatre and the world's largest crayfish party.

MALMÖ

SEE
Malmö Konsthall..........1 C4
Malmöhus Slott............2 A2
Moderna Museet
Malmo.........................3 D2

SHOP
Form/Design Center......4 C2
Olssen & Gerthel..........5 B2
Toffelmakaren...............6 C2

EAT
Bastard.........................7 B2
Victors.........................8 C2
Årstiderna i Kockska
Huset...........................9 C2

DRINK
Belle Epoque..............10 D5
Solde..........................11 C3
Tempo Bar & Kök........12 D5

PLAY
Debaser......................13 D5
Kulturbolaget..............14 D5
Rundan Canal Tour......15 C2

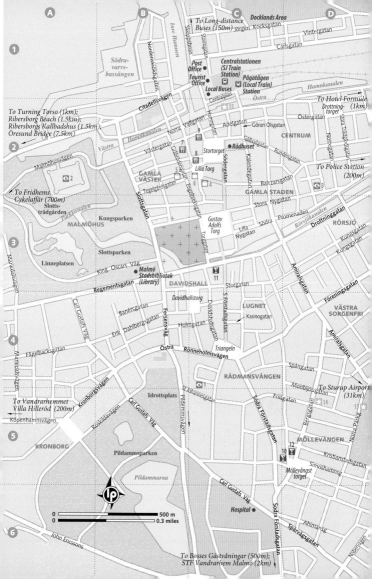

A B C D

1

Södra-
varvs-
bassängen

To Long-distance
Buses (150m)

Docklands Area
Jörgen Kocksgatan

Carlsgatan

Vintergatan

Nordenskiöldsgatan

Post
Office
Tourist
Office

Centralstationen
(SJ Train
Station)
Local Buses
Centralplan

Pågatågen
(Local Train)
Station
Östra

Hamnkanalen

To Hotel Formule
(1km)

Drottning-
torget

Östergatan

To Turning Torso (1km);
Ribersborg Beach (1.5km);
Ribersborgs Kallbadshus (1.5km);
Öresund Bridge (7.5km)

Citadellsvägen

CENTRUM

2

Norra Vallgatan

Hamnkanalen

Adelgatan

Göran Olsgatan

Västra

Västergatan

Stortorget

Rådhuset

Rundelgatan

To Police Station
(200m)

Malmöhusvägen

GAMLA
VÄSTER

Lilla Torg

Södergatan

Kalendegatan

Baltzarsgatan

GAMLA STADEN

Stora Nygatan

Promenaden

To Fridhems
Cykelaffär (700m)
Slotts-
trädgården

Tegelgårdsgatan

Kungsparken

Slottsgatan

Gustav
Adolfs
Torg

Lilla
Nygatan

Södra

Rörsjökanalen

Drottninggatan

RÖRSJÖ

MALMÖHUS

Parkkanalen

King Oscars Väg

Malmö
Stadsbibliotek
(Library)

Kungsgatan

3

Slottsparken

DAVIDSHALL

11

Storgatan

Amiralsgatan

Föreningsgatan

Linneplatsen

Regementsgatan

Davidhallstorg

Davidhallsgatan

LUGNET

Kasinogatan

VÄSTRA
SORGENFRI

Banérsgatan

Erik Dahlbergsgatan

Fersensvägen

Holmgatan

Triangeln

Amiralsgatan

Fågelbacksgatan

Carl Gustafs Väg

Östra
Rönneholmsvägen

RÅDMANSVÅNGEN

Spångatan

To Sturup Airport
(31km)

4

Mariedalsvägen

Idrottsplats

St Knänsgatan

Monbijougatan

Friisgatan

14

To Vandrarhemmet
Villa Hilleröd (200m)

Kronborgsvägen

Carl Gustaf Väg

Pildammsvägen

Södra Förstadsgatan

Bergsgatan

MÖLLEVÅNGEN

Rödkullavägen

KRONBORG

Köpenhamnsvägen

Pildammsparken

Pildammarna

Carl Gustafs Väg

12

10

Möllevångs
torget

Kristianstadsgatan

Simrishamnsgatan

5

Mariedalsvägen

IP

0   500 m
0   0.3 miles

Hospital

Södra Förstadsgatan

Spårvägsgatan

Nobelvägen

Ahlmansg

6

John Ericssons

To Bosses Gästvåningar (500m);
STF Vandrarhem Malmö (2km)

⊙ SEE

◉ MALMÖ KONSTHALL

☎ 040 34 12 86; www.konsthall.malmo
.se; St Johannesgatan 7; admission free;
⏲ 11am-5pm Mon-Tue & Thu-Sun, to
9pm Wed; 🚌 8, 2, 5

One of Europe's largest art spaces
dedicated to contemporary art,
this place has permanent and
temporary exhibitions.

◉ MALMÖHUS SLOTT

☎ 040 34 44 00; www.malmo.se/
museer; Malmöhusvägen; adult/child
under 7yr/7-15yr 40/free/10Skr; ⏲ 10am-
4pm Mon-Fri, noon-4pm Sat & Sun Sep-
May, 10am-4pm daily Jun-Aug; 🚌 3

Malmö's 15th-century castle is
home to a small Naturmuseet
(Natural History Museum), Malmö
Konstmuseum (Art Museum) and
the Stadsmuseet (City Museum).

Behind is the lovely, landscaped
Kungsparken (the King's park),
with its waterways, gardens and
picnic areas.

◉ MODERNA MUSEET
MALMÖ

☎ 040 68 57 937; www.moderna
museet.se; Gasverksgatan 22; adult/child
under 18yr/concession 80/free/60Skr;
⏲ 11am-6pm Tue & Thu-Sun, to 9pm
Wed

This smaller outpost of Stockholm's iconic modern art museum
occupies an early 20th-century
power station, complete with
a bold perforated extension by
Swedish firm Tham & Videgård
Arkitekter. Three major exhibitions
are held annually, with recent
shows including provocative video
art from Israeli artist Yael Bartana.

Discover the history of Malmö within the museums of Malmöhus Slott

TELEPHONE CODES AND CURRENCY
The international dialling code for Sweden is 46, while Malmö's local code is (0) 40. Generally one Danish krone equals 1.24 Swedish kroner (Skr).

☉ RIBERSBORGS KALLBADHUS

☎ 040 26 03 66; www.ribersborgskall-badhus.se; Ribersborg Stranden; adult/child 7-17yr 55/30Skr; ☽ 9am-8pm Mon, Tue, Thu, Fri, to 9pm Wed, to 6pm Sat & Sun May-Aug, 10am-7pm Mon, Tue, Thu, Fri, to 8pm Wed, 9am-4pm Sat & Sun Sep-Apr; ☐ 3
This rickety wooden pier, dating from 1898, offers an opportunity to enjoy the invigorating, uniquely Scandinavian experience of a wood-fired sauna (with separate male and female sections), followed by a bracing dip in the sea.

☉ TURNING TORSO

Västra Varvsgatan, Western Harbour; ☐ 2
This controversial, 190m-high residential and conference tower was completed in November 2005 and stands in the heart of the rapidly expanding 'docklands' of Malmö's western harbour. Based on a work of sculpture by the architect himself, Spaniard Santiago Calatrava, the tower's 54 storeys twist 90 degrees as they climb upwards, creating an extraordinary effect – particularly if you stand at its base. The tower is not open to the gen-

eral public but there is a gallery and small shopping centre next door.

🛍 SHOP

Malmö's main shopping area is the pedestrian Södergatan, which begins at Stortorget and runs through the city centre to Gustav Adolfs Torg. From here the shops continue along Södra Förstads-gatan to Triangeln. It is all a bit provincial compared to Copenhagen, but there are some other good areas to investigate: the small but cute old town, Gamla Väster, to the west of Lilla Torg; Adelgaten and Östergatan; and the area further south, Möllevångstorget (known locally as Möllan, or 'the windmill'), with its numerous Asian grocery stores. Shopping hours are, generally, 10am to 6pm or 7pm from Monday to Friday, 10am to 3pm on Saturday and – Copenhageners take note – some shops also open noon to 4pm on Sunday.

⬜ FORM/DESIGN CENTER
Design/Homewares
☎ 040 664 51 50; www.formdesign center.com; ☽ 11am-5pm Tue, Wed & Fri, to 6pm Thu, to 4pm Sat, noon-4pm Sun
The exhibition space on the first floor of this historic warehouse just off Lilla Torg is dedicated to mainly Swedish design and architecture. There is a café and shop selling a range of cleverly designed clothing, textiles and homewares on the second floor.

🏠 OLSSON & GERTHEL
Homewares

☎ 040 611 7000; www.olssongerthel
.se; Engelbrektsgatan 9; ⏰ 11am-6pm
Mon-Fri, to 3pm Sat

One of the best interior design and
homeware shops in the city is just
a couple of seconds away from
Lilla Torg and stocks delectable
European brands, including the
adorable Italian Robex plasticware
and Stelton gifts, plus lighting,
silverware, Tivoli Audio and locally
made ceramics. Just across the
road is another design shop, **For-
margruppen** (same opening hours),
selling glassware, ceramics and
arts and crafts.

🏠 TOFFELMAKAREN *Footwear*

☎ 040 23 22 45; www.toffelmakaren.
se; Lilla Torg 9; ⏰ 10am-6pm Mon-Fri,
to 3pm Sat

This little store sells traditional
and modern handmade clogs
fashioned from alder tree and fine
leather. It could hold the answer to
all your gift needs, assuming you
know the shoe size of your giftees.

🍴 EAT

Lilla Torg is the mainstream hub
for bars and restaurants with Indian, Italian, Japanese, French and
Swedish cuisines all represented
on this pretty, cobbled square.
The atmosphere in Lilla Torg on a
Friday or Saturday night is flirty,
friendly, a bit boisterous and loads
of fun. But younger, hipper locals
tend to shun Lilla Torg in favour of
the area around Möllevångstorget,
which has cooler DJ bars with
cheaper drinks and food.

🍴 BASTARD
Modern European   €€€

☎ 040 12 13 18; www.bastardrestaurant
.se; Mäster Johansgatan 11; ⏰ 5pm-
midnight Tue-Thu, to 2am Fri & Sat

Complete with backyard bar, eye-
candy waiters and camp baronial
touches, the seasonal menu at
convivial Bastard covers three
categories: Cold, Wood-Fired, and
From the Oven. Devour anything
from creamy *burrata* cheese on
grilled fennel to soul-warming ox-
tail and tongue pie with chanterelle
mushrooms and broad beans.

▮▮ VICTORS *Swedish* €€€
☎ 040 12 76 70; Lilla Torg 1; 11.30am-10.30pm Mon-Sat

This Lilla Torg landmark serves well-priced Swedish staples and transforms into a DJ bar by night. Victors has an authentic Swedish style, with stark wood panelling and simple, sturdy, minimalist furniture.

▮▮ ÅRSTIDERNA I KOCKSKA HUSET
Classic Franco-Swedish €€€
☎ 040 230 910; www.arstiderna.se; Frans Suellsgatan 3; 🕑 11.30am-midnight Mon-Fri, 5pm-midnight Sat

This enchanting 16th-century red-brick cellar restaurant with its vaulted ceilings and cosy corners has been considered the ultimate Malmö gourmet destination for years. And it lives up to its billing, serving seriously impeccable French-inspired food, such as fillet of veal with sweetbreads in a port wine sauce flavoured with duck's liver. Exemplary service and luscious – mostly French and Italian – wines make this every bit as good as Copenhagen's finest.

▶ DRINK

Sweden's Draconian licensing laws mean that, aside from the government-run alcohol shops, you can only buy alcohol in restaurants, bars and hotels. The main nightlife areas are Lilla Torg, the streets around Möllevång-storget and upcoming bar haven Davidhallstorg.

▶ BELLE EPOQUE
Bar/Restaurant
☎ 040 973 990; Södra Skolgatan 43; 🕑 6pm-1am Tue-Sat

Though new on the scene, retro-chic Belle Epoque has wasted little time building a solid rep. It swooped street press *Nojesguiden*'s 'Best Bar' award in 2009, while its French-inspired bistro grub has already made it into Swedish gourmet bible, the *White Guide*. The wines (all from small producers) include a number of interesting organic drops, while the choice of indie brews includes Newcastle Brown Ale, Duvel and San Francisco's Anchor Steam. Soak it all up with fresh, seasonal, weekly changing dishes including Atlantic cod with lemongrass, celeriac, melon, mint and parmesan, or zucchini with chickpeas and paprika.

▶ SOLDE *Cafe*
☎ 040 692 80 87; Regementsgatan 3; 🕑 7.15am-6.30pm Mon-Fri, 9am-4pm Sat

Malmö's coolest cafe is a grit-hip combo of concrete bar, white-tiled walls, art exhibitions and creative media regulars. Owner Johan Carlström is an award-winning

MALMÖ TRAVEL
> Distance from Copenhagen – 30km
> Direction – West
> Travel time – 35 minutes

The best way to travel to Malmö is by train. Trains leave every 20 minutes from Copenhagen Central Station to Malmö station, via Copenhagen Airport, from 5am to midnight and hourly through the night (www.dsb.dk). You can also drive, but the Øresund bridge toll for cars is quite steep (375kr each way). To reach the bridge, head south out of the city, through Christianshavn and Amager, following signs along Amagerstrandvej to Copenhagen Airport. Just before the airport, signs will send you west towards the water and Malmö.

barista; watch him in action over lip-smacking Italian panini, biscotti and *cornetti* (croissants).

☎ TEMPO BAR & KÖK *Bar*
☎ 040 126 021; Södra Skolegatan 30; 🕙 5pm-midnight Mon & Tue, to 1am Wed & Thu, 4pm-1am Fri & Sat, to 11pm Sun; 🚌 8, 2, 5
This ever-lively bar-restaurant remains a popular evening hang-out for loyal locals. Once known for its DJ-sets, the focus has since turned to fine-tuning the food, dubbed *husmanskost* (traditional Swedish home cooking) with a twist. Close to Möllevångstorget, it's popular with students and creative types.

⭐ PLAY

⭐ DEBASER *Live Music/Club*
☎ 040 239 880; www.debaser.se; Norra Parkgatan 2; admission free to 10pm, then 100Skr; 🕙 7am-3am Wed-Sat, brunch 11am-3pm Sun
Stockholm's music club heavyweight opened shop in Malmö a

few years ago. Still going strong, it's a head-nodding combo of live gigs and club nights spanning anything from indie, pop and hip-hop, to soul, electronica and rock. There's a buzzing outdoor bar-lounge overlooking Folkets Park and decent grub (carnivores shouldn't miss the chilli burger) till 10pm for a pre-party feed.

⭐ KULTURBOLAGET *Club*
☎ 040 302 011; www.kulturbolaget .se; Bergsgatan 18; opening hours & prices vary
The mainstay of the city's music-based nightlife scene is this 750-capacity live-music and club venue that hosts big international acts – Morrissey, Emmy-lou Harris – and heavily popular club nights on Fridays and Saturdays.

⭐ RUNDAN CANAL TOURS *Tours*
☎ 040 611 74 88; www.rundan.se; adult/ child 110/55kr; 🕙 hourly 11am-4pm Apr

WORTH THE TRIP

Within cannon range of Sweden on the Danish side of the Øresund, further north from Malmö, lies Denmark's most imposing castle, **Kronborg Slot** (☎ 49 21 30 78; www.kronborg.dk; adult/child under 6yr/6-14yr 75/free/25kr; 🕐 11am-3pm Tue-Sun Jan-Mar, Nov & Dec, 11am-4pm Tue-Sun Apr & Oct, 10.30am-5pm May-Sep; 🚇 Helsingør, then 10-min walk). Known to the world as Elsinore Castle and home to Shakespeare's *Hamlet*, Kronborg was built here at the entrance to the Øresund and Baltic as a grandiose tollhouse, to extract money from ships passing between the coasts of Denmark and Sweden, and as a defensive post against fleets sailing on Copenhagen. The so-called Sound Dues were introduced in the 1420s by King Erik of Pomerania. He built a small fortress, Krogen, here to operate the toll. Frederik II rebuilt and enlarged the castle in a Renaissance style between 1574 and 1585 and Christian IV rebuilt it again after a fire in 1629. In 1658 the Swedes occupied the castle and took virtually everything of value from it. It was converted into barracks in 1785 and fulfilled this role until 1922, when it was opened to the public.

Today you can see the stunning 62m ballroom and other royal rooms, as well as visit the casemates and Denmark's national Maritime Museum. A stroll on the ramparts comes free of charge and, on a blue-skied spring morning, is wonderfully bracing. During the summer, Kronborg pays its respects to its most famous – largely fictional – resident, William Shakespeare's troubled teen, Hamlet. Shakespeare wrote his longest piece in 1602; scholars believe it was based on the eyewitness reports of other English actors who had visited it (there is no evidence that Shakespeare ever came here, although some of his descriptions of the castle are strikingly evocative), although two characters, Rosencrantz and Guildenstern, took their names from real Danish noblemen who had visited the English court in 1590. Every summer the castle hosts an outdoor production of the play. In the past Laurence Olivier, Richard Burton, Kenneth Branagh and Simon Russel Beale have all 'played the Dane' here.

Driving from Copenhagen, the quickest way to Helsingør is to head north on the E47/E55. But far nicer is to take the coast road, Strandvejen (route 152), which winds through the posh villas and small beaches along the exclusive Øresund coast north of the city. DSB trains to and from Copenhagen run roughly three times an hour from early morning to around midnight. Journey time is 55 minutes. If you're day-tripping it from Copenhagen, buy a '24-timer billet' (24hr ticket, adult/child 130/65kr) from the ticket vending machines at the station.

29-Jun 22, to 7pm Jun 24-Aug 27, to 3pm Aug 28-Sep 17, noon-2pm Sep 18-Oct 1, additional 75min 9pm tour Jul 18-Aug 17 These tour boats depart on a 50-minute guided tour of the canal that circles the centre of Malmö from just opposite the Central Station and includes commentary. Tours leave every hour on the hour.

For such a small city Copenhagen has a terrific range of things to offer visitors – from a burgeoning food scene and superb accomodation options, to freewheeling travel by bike and one of the best jazz festivals in the world.

Jazz musician in Nyhavn

SNAPSHOTS

ACCOMMODATION

Copenhagen is enjoying a hotel boom. Room numbers have risen by more than 40% over the last half-decade to a total of more than 15,000 today. The main growth has been in the midpriced places (800kr to 2000kr), but the bargain end (450kr to 800kr) has also seen considerable growth. This is not the dauntingly expensive city to stay in that it used to be.

The budget hotel area is centred on the western side of the Central Station, around Vesterbrogade and the fruitier parts of Istedgade. Slightly pricier places are to be found on and close to Rådhuspladsen while most of the posher, four- and five-star places are on the eastern side of the city centre, around Kongens Nytorv, Bredgade and the harbour.

Styles range from the experimental design of Hotel Fox, where each room is designed by a different artist (to often freaky effect), to the chintzy luxury of the celebs' favourite, the five-star Hotel d'Angleterre, and the cool, contemporary Scandinavian design of the glamorous Sankt Petri. Towering over them all is the Radisson SAS Royal, designed down to its doorknobs by Denmark's master builder, Arne Jacobsen.

The Cab-Inn chain (www.cabinn.com) has revolutionised budget accommodation in the city in recent years and has four hotels (although only the Cab-Inn City can truly be termed 'central'), with rooms from 485kr per person. Cab-Inn's latest rival is Wakeup Copenhagen (www.wakeupcopenhagen.com), a sleek two-star option with designer Danish furniture and rooms from 400kr per person. Within walking distance of Central Station, Tivoli and the waterfront, it's also close to huge 'designer' hostel Danhostel Copenhagen City (www.danhostel.dk), another sound budget option.

lonely planet Hotels & Hostels

Need a place to stay? Find and book it at lonelyplanet.com. There are many properties featured for Copenhagen – each personally visited, thoroughly reviewed and happily recommended by a Lonely Planet author. From hostels to high-end hotels, we've hunted out the places that will bring you unique and special experiences. Read independent reviews by authors and other travellers, and get practical information including amenities, maps and photos. Then reserve your room simply and securely via Hotels & Hostels – our online booking service. It's all at lonelyplanet.com/hotels.

The Square
COPENHAGEN

BEST
> Hotel d'Angleterre (www.remmen.dk)
> Hotel Sankt Petri (www.hotelsktpetri.dk)
> Radisson SAS Royal (www.radisson.com)
> Hotel Fox (www.hotelfox.dk)
> Square (www.thesquarecopenhagen.com)
> Hotel Front (www.front.dk)

BEST FOR THE AIRPORT
> Hilton Copenhagen Airport (www.hilton.com)

BEST BUDGET
> Wakeup Copenhagen (www.wakeupcopenhagen.com)
> Danhostel Copenhagen City (www.danhostel.dk)

BEST VALUE WITH CHARACTER
> Hotel Guldsmeden chain (www.hotelguldsmeden.dk)

Opposite The exterior of the luxurious Hotel d'Angleterre **Above** View from a stylish room at the Square

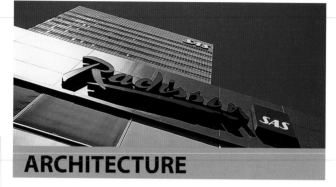

ARCHITECTURE

Copenhagen's architectural story begins at Slotsholmen and Bishop Absalon's 12th-century fortress. You can still see its ruins under Christiansborg Slot (p72).

In the early 17th century Christian IV's extraordinary building program saw the construction of the elaborately embellished Børsen (the Stock Exchange; p74), Rundetårn (p11) and Rosenborg Slot (p120) – although at a great cost.

The ornate baroque style was a popular design for public building in the later 17th century and two splendid buildings representative of the style are Vor Frelsers Kirke (p96) in Christianshavn, and Charlottenborg (p81) at Kongens Nytorv, a former palace that now houses an art gallery.

Pre-eminent among the city's rococo structures are Amalienborg Slot's (p80) four nearly identical mansions, which were designed by architect Nicolai Eigtved at the end of the 18th century. The buildings are the residence of the royal family, but one of them is accessible to the public as a museum.

The city's leading architect of the late 19th century was Vilhelm Dahlerup, who borrowed from a broad spectrum of European Renaissance influences. His most remarkable works include Ny Carlsberg Glyptotek (p42) and the ornate Det Kongelige Teater (p90).

Some of the grander neoclassical buildings of the period are Vor Frue Kirke (p56) in the Latin Quarter and the city courthouse Domhuset (p51) on Nytorv.

Arne Jacobsen (1902–71) was a Copenhagen native and spent most of his life in his beloved city. His best-known architectural effort is the Radisson SAS Royal Hotel (p60), but he also designed the Dansk National Bank Building at Holmens Canal and a petrol station on Kystvejen in Charlottenlund, which still pumps petrol today.

The leading architect from the present day is Henning Larsen. His work includes the five-storey Dansk Design Center (p42) and the impressionists wing of the Ny Carlsberg Glyptotek. In January 2005 Copenhagen's new Opera House (p100) opened. Also by Larsen, this dazzling building features a 32m-long cantilever and six theatres.

Equally dramatic is the Royal Library extension (p75), dubbed the 'Black Diamond' (Den Sorte Diamant), which has a striking façade of black granite and smoked glass and a brilliant use of internal space. It was designed by Schmidt, Hammer and Lassen.

If you'd like to get more information about local architecture, visit the Dansk Arkitektur Center at Gammel Dok (p95).

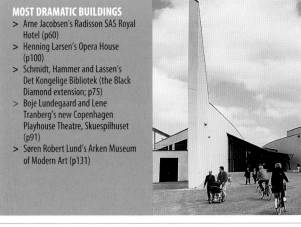

MOST DRAMATIC BUILDINGS
> Arne Jacobsen's Radisson SAS Royal Hotel (p60)
> Henning Larsen's Opera House (p100)
> Schmidt, Hammer and Lassen's Det Kongelige Bibliotek (the Black Diamond extension; p75)
> Boje Lundegaard and Lene Tranberg's new Copenhagen Playhouse Theatre, Skuespilhuset (p91)
> Soren Robert Lund's Arken Museum of Modern Art (p131)

Opposite The attention-seeking Radisson SAS Royal **Above** The oblique angles of the Arken Museum of Modern Art

CYCLING

Copenhagen is one of the best cities in Europe for getting around by bicycle. There are separate cycle lanes along all of the main roads in Copenhagen and cycle racks everywhere you go, too. Three out of four Danes own bicycles and half use them on a regular basis.

Visitors needn't feel left out. From April to November, 2000 free City Bikes are available at 110 bike racks located around the city centre. To deter theft and minimise maintenance, the bicycles have a distinctive design that includes solid spokeless wheels with puncture-resistant tyres. You deposit a 20kr coin in the stand to release the bike. When you've finished using the bicycle, you can return it to any stand and get your 20kr back.

Bikes can be carried free on S-trains but are banned at Nørreport station from 7.30am to 8.30am and 3.30 to 5pm weekdays. On the metro, bikes are banned from 7am to 9am and 3.30pm to 5.30pm, and require a bike ticket, purchased from ticket machines. Load your bicycle into any carriage with a cycle symbol; you must stay with the bike at all times.

There are some rules worth knowing when cycling in Denmark. Cyclists give way to passengers crossing cycle lanes when embarking or disembarking at bus stops but pretty much everyone else is supposed to give way to cyclists. Cars turning right must wait for cyclists to pass them on the inside (though they obviously can't be relied upon to do this), but cyclists are not allowed to make left turns at traffic lights and larger junctions – they are supposed to dismount and cross with pedestrians before remounting and continuing.

Cycling maps, including a 1:100,000-scale map of North Zealand (covering the greater Copenhagen area), are produced by Dansk Cyklist Forbund (Danish Cycling Federation; www.dcf.dk) and can be purchased at bookshops. For bicycle hire, see p171.

KIDS

If the very thought of a city break with young children has you reaching for the Valium, Copenhagen has the solution. Everywhere you go the city appears to have been geared to the little angels. Virtually all the restaurants have highchairs and many have children's menus. All the main museums offer buggies to visitors, the transport system can accommodate the largest of prams (indeed, you will notice that the Danes love those big, old Victorian-style contraptions) and there are superb play areas in all the parks. Many museums have children's sections, the theatres and music venues often have children's productions and concerts and we haven't even started on the sights and attractions created specifically for children, like the remarkable Experimentarium (p104).

The long list of kid-friendly options would surely be headed by Tivoli (p44), which has to be one of the most charming fun parks in the world. It has something for children of all ages, from pulse-quickening rollercoasters and shooting galleries to sedate carousels and tea-cup rides. A visit to Tivoli can be an expensive affair, but there are plenty of free shows, including the famous historic Comedia dell'Arte theatre, the fireworks (if the kids can stay up till close to midnight) and the amazing night-time lighting displays. It's also worth checking out the Buster children's film festival (www.buster.dk), which overtakes city cinemas in mid-September.

BEST FOR KIDS
> Tivoli (p44)
> Zoologisk Have (p129)
> Rundetårn (p11)
> Kongens Have (p119)
> Bakken (p107)

BEST FOR A RAINY DAY
> DGI-Byen (p135)
> Imax Tycho Brahe Planetarium (p135)
> Zoologisk Museum (p105)
> Experimentarium (p104)
> Nationalmuseet (p42)

SNAPSHOTS

HYGGE

We realise it is a little unusual for a guidebook to dedicate a full page to a feeling, but in the case of the Danish *hygge* we heartily recommend that you grab a bit of the action. So what is *hygge*? Usually it is translated as 'cosy' but *hygge* means much more than that. *Hygge* refers to a sense of friendly, warm companionship of a kind fostered when Danes gather together in groups of two or more, although you can actually *hygge* yourself if there is no one else around. The participants don't even have to be friends (indeed, you might only just have met), but if the conversation flows – avoiding potentially divisive topics like politics and the best method to pickle herring – the bonhomie blossoms, toasts are raised before an open fire (or, at the very least, some candles), you are probably coming close. Happily, Copenhagen's restaurants, cafes and bars do their utmost to foster a *hyggelige* atmosphere, with open fires, candles lit no matter what time of day or year and, of course, a nonstop supply of alcohol (which is sold in virtually all cafes). Listed below are some of the best places to experience that *hygge* vibe.

BEST HYGGE CAFES

> Bastionen og Løven (p98)
> Dyrehaven (p131)
> La Glace (p66)
> Tea Time (p113; pictured right)
> Café Wilder (p98)

BEST HYGGE BARS

> Bibendum (p124)
> Bankeråt (p122)
> Palæ Bar (p90)
> Falernum (p134)
> Harbo Bar (p111)

SHOPPING

What Copenhagen's shopping portfolio lacks in size it more than makes up for with quality and individuality. If you are bored with mass-produced, chain store designs, the side streets and offbeat shopping areas of the city have the answer. Of course, Copenhagen has all the big retail names and some homegrown heavyweights – Illums Bolighus (p62), Georg Jensen (p59) and Bang & Olufsen (p84) among them – which are mostly centred on the main pedestrian shopping street, Strøget. However, the city's real strength lies in its young designers, working alone or in small collectives and selling their clothes, interior design items, ceramics and glassware from their own shops. They're predominantly in Vesterbro (p126) and Nørrebro (p102), but also in the areas north and south of Strøget between Kongens Nytorv and Købmagergade, and on Strædet (p55).

The first thing you need to know about shopping in Copenhagen is that, as fantastic as its shops are, shopping is very much a privilege, not a right, in Denmark. There are strict laws governing how many hours and days a week shops can open and, as difficult as it might be to deal with for those used to the 24/7 spending opportunities in London or New York, most shops close early on Saturdays and few, aside from local grocers, ever open on a Sunday. That said, many shops do stay open late (until 7pm or 8pm) on Fridays. And for Sunday shopping, there is always Malmö (p138).

Visitors from countries outside the EU who buy goods in Denmark can get a refund of the 25% VAT, less a handling fee, if they spend at least 300kr at any retail outlet that participates in the 'Tax Free Shopping Global Refund' plan. This includes most shops catering for tourists. The 300kr can be spent on a single item or several items as long as they are purchased from the same shop. Visit www.globalrefund.com for more information.

MUSIC

Copenhagen has a small, lively music scene with some impressive venues, all offering a wide range of classical, jazz, opera, pop and rock music. You can catch a live-music performance of some sort or other most nights of the week, whether it be a late-night jazz jam at La Fontaine (p71), a lavish, cutting edge Cosi Fan Tutti at the Opera House (p100) or a major chart star at Vega (p135). Major international acts such as Madonna and Bob Dylan have recently taken to playing in Jutland over the capital, but venues such as Forum (p135) and the national stadium Parken (p115) still attract big stars.

In terms of homegrown acts, Denmark's biggest-selling piece of music ever is 'Barbie Girl' by the blessedly defunct Aqua, which sold 28 million copies in the late 1990s. It was the first major international hit by a Danish artist since Whigfield's 'Saturday Night', which wasn't exactly a track record to be proud of, but a small trickle of better-quality Danish acts have followed, including Kashmir (often compared to Radiohead), Tim Christensen (a talented folk-rock singer-songwriter), the Raveonettes (Denmark's answer to the White Stripes) and prog-rock outfit Mew, all of whom have enjoyed significant overseas sales in recent years. The Danish DJ and remix scene is centred on Copenhagen and is buoyant with acts such as SoulShock, Cutfather and Junior Senior achieving some success abroad.

The **Roskilde Festival** (www.roskilde-festival.dk; 🕥 30 Jun-3 Jul 2011, 5-8 Jul 2012) in 2010 saw acts as diverse as Prince, Patti Smith and Gorillaz, not to mention a large range of Scandinavian bands, take the stage; 2011 features Kings of Leon and Iron Maiden. Standard tickets including camping cost 1725kr in 2011; check the website for the latest details. See p20 and p26.

TOP FIVE COPENHAGEN SOUNDTRACKS

> 'Wonderful Copenhagen' (Danny Kaye) Don't pretend you haven't been singing this to yourself since you got here...
> 'Barbie Girl' (Aqua) As soothing as a foghorn and as subtle as a brick, it remains one of Denmark's biggest global hits.
> 'Love in a Trashcan' (The Raveonettes) The lead single from the duo's 2005 album *Pretty in Black*.
> 'Played-A-Live (The Bongo Song)' (Safri Duo). Idiotic drum anthem from the classically trained Danish percussionists, who ought to know better.
> 'Fly on the Wings of Love' (Olsen Brothers) 2000 Eurovision winner. Denmark's proudest moment since... well, possibly ever.

JAZZ

Jazz arrived in Copenhagen in the mid-1920s and it didn't take long for a strong local scene to grow up around the clubs in the city. Major international jazz stars such as Louis Armstrong and Django Reinhardt were drawn to the Danish capital by its enthusiastic, knowledgeable audiences; Stan Getz, Dexter Gordon and Ben Webster even lived in the city during the peak of their careers. After WWII Copenhagen came to be considered the jazz capital of Scandinavia and its legendary Montmartre Club was one of the most famous jazz venues in Europe. Closed for years, Montmartre reopened as Jazzhus Montmartre (p71) in July 2010 at its original site, adding more muscle to a scene that includes the intimate, equally historic La Fontaine (p71), as well as smaller venues such as Huset (p70).

Many of the city's other music venues such as Tivoli's Koncertsal (p49) and even the Opera House (p100) turn their hand to jazz from time to time – particularly during July's Copenhagen Jazz Festival (p21), but one of the true titans of the city's jazz scene today remains the Copenhagen Jazzhouse (p69), located just north of central Strøget. This two-storey venue hosts live performances encompassing a wide range of jazz genres and featuring international and domestic stars, often followed by club nights on the intimate basement dance floor. Together with Vega (p135) it is one of the most consistent live-music venues in the city.

Copenhagen is still home to a large group of both homegrown and international jazz musicians. The living legend of the Copenhagen jazz scene is 91-year-old Svend Asmussen, who has played with the likes of Benny Goodman, Fats Waller and Django Reinhardt in his time. He still plays in Copenhagen occasionally, as does veteran trumpeter Palle Mikkelborg. If you are interested in learning more about the jazz scene in Copenhagen and taking in a few clubs, you might enjoy a Copenhagen Jazz Tour (p178).

BEST JAZZ VENUES

> Copenhagen Jazzhouse (www .copenhagenjazzhouse.dk)
> La Fontaine (www.lafontaine.dk)
> Jazzhus Montmartre (www .jazzhusmontmartre.dk)
> Huset (www.huset.dk)
> Vega (www.vega.dk; pictured right)

SEASONAL COPENHAGEN

With weather as extreme as Copenhagen's can be, the seasons can have a significant impact on a visit. That is not to say you shouldn't come here in the winter; there are pluses as well as minuses at this time of year, particularly at Christmas time. Copenhagen lays on a fantastic Christmas: the decorations come out on Strøget's shopping strips, Tivoli (p44) opens with its special brand of seasonal schmaltz and the cafes do a roaring trade in mulled red wine and roaring fires. Heavy snow rarely hinders the locals from getting on with things, so you needn't worry about finding yourself hotel-bound, just do make sure you have enough clothing with you. We don't want to sound like your mother here, but you can get some excellent winter sports clothing in the outdoors shops on Frederiksborggade and there is nothing like an Icelandic woollen to keep the chill out. From the end of November to February you can practise your figure eights at open-air ice-skating rinks in Frederiksberg Runddel, Blågårds Plads in Nørrebro and Toftegårds Plads in suburban Valby.

That said, most people seem to agree that the best time to visit Copenhagen is between May and August. As soon as the sun starts to radiate a little warmth, an extraordinary change comes over the city. The locals cast off their clothes, take to the outdoor cafe tables en masse and, at the weekend, really let their hair down with numerous festivals (p24), outdoor music and, it has to be said, liver-shrivelling amounts of alcohol. They even go swimming in the harbour (see p100). Be warned: Copenhagen does go a little dead in late July, when the entire city seems to leave for their summer houses and some of the better restaurants close.

ROMANTIC COPENHAGEN

It takes a lot to maintain a façade of romance when the temperature is touching -15°C, you're up to your knees in slushy, muddy snow and you're wrapped up like the Michelin Man, but somehow, against the odds, Copenhagen is a deeply romantic city, even in winter. Consider a walk through a frosty Dyrehaven (p107), then back to town for a mulled wine beside the open fire in Cap Horn (p85), and dinner at Alberto K (p46) as you watch the lights in Sweden gently twinkling. Come springtime and the options multiply exponentially, not least because you can now dress like a human instead of a walrus. The cafés and restaurants move their tables outside, the flowers blossom in Frederiksberg Have (p128) and the Jazz Festival (p21) gives you all the excuse you need to sweep your lover up in to your arms and spin him/her around the dance floor.

BEST ROMANTIC RESTAURANTS
> Alberto K (p46)
> Orangeriet (p122)
> Paul (p47)
> Restaurant d'Angleterre (p89)
> Les Trois Cochons (p132)

BEST ROMANTIC WALKS
> Tivoli (p44), but only after dark
> Kongens Have (p119), but not if the sunbathers are out
> Frederiksberg Have (p128), but only if it's springtime
> Dyrehaven (p107), but only when it's frosty
> Langelinie to the Little Mermaid (p82), but only if the wind isn't blowing

V

SNAPSHOTS

TRADITIONAL FOOD

For all the hype and hullabaloo surrounding modern Scandinavian cooking, the truth is that most Danes are a conservative bunch when it comes to food. Even though Copenhageners – particularly the younger ones – are dining out more and more, their compatriots generally prefer homecooked, stout fare. Dishes heavy on pork are invariably accompanied by potatoes in one form or another, and *brun sovs*, a kind of gravy. *Frikadeller*, the traditional Danish meatball, are a mixture of minced beef and pork eaten by every Dane at least a couple of times a month. Meanwhile, pickled herring *(sild)*, remains the staple of the *kolde bord* (cold table, Denmark's answer to the Swedish smorgasbord).

As you might have guessed, the Danish diet is not an especially healthy one. They eat large quantities of animal fats, processed foods and dairy produce. Breakfast often consists of pastries, cheese and cured meats. Traditionally, the favourite fast food is hot dogs from the *pølser vogner* (sausage wagons) that station themselves around the city, all churning out precisely the same frankfurter, buns and dressings (although, we have to admit, occasionally a *pølser* slathered with fake mustard and ketchup can really hit the spot). Interesting foodstuffs to try or take home include pickled herring, salami, smoked fish, local cheeses and akvavit, the 40%-proof herbed potato spirit, which does a good job of numbing the palate before you eat.

BEST FOR TRADITIONAL DANISH FOOD

> Schønnemann (p66)
> Slotskælderen Hos Gitte Kik (p67)
> Aamanns Takeaway (p121)
> Cap Horn (p85)
> Andersen Bakery Hot Dog Kiosk (p47)

NEW FOOD

A few years ago Copenhagen would have been the last place on earth to recommend food-lovers to visit. Today Copenhagen has more Michelin stars than any other Scandinavian city. What has turned this culinary backwater into a burgeoning culinary destination?

The answer is: its young chefs, many of whom have trained at prestigious, progressive restaurants around Europe and the US. These chefs, including Noma's (p99) René Redzepi and Mielcke & Hurtigkarl's (p133) Jakob Mielcke, have taken their experience and combined it with a passion for Denmark's local raw ingredients – its excellent pork, game, seafood, wild mushrooms, berries etc – and an almost religious observance of the seasons. One measure of the new seriousness with which Danes approach the business of food is the instant success of their first food festival, Copenhagen Cooking (p28). Fresh arrivals on the Copenhagen dining scene include seafood darling Kødbyens Fiskebar (p132), whimsical Orangeriet (p122) and restaurateur Christian Aarø's Restaurant AOC (p89), awarded its first Michelin star in 2010. So the New Danish food revolution is in full swing and that can only be good news for tourists, particularly as the number of places with outdoor seating has almost quadrupled in the last decade. One benefit, at least, of global warming.

BEST FOR MODERN NORDIC COOKING
> Noma (p99)
> Restaurant AOC (p89)
> Mielcke & Hurtigkarl (p133)

BEST DÉCOR
> Kødbyens Fiskebar (p132)
> Mielcke & Hurtigkarl (p133)

BEST FOREIGN
> Damindra (p87)
> Kiin Kiin (p110)
> Fischer (p109)
> Sticks 'n' Sushi (p122)

BEST BUDGET
> Café Ñ (p108)
> Andersen Bakery Hot Dog Kiosk (p47)
> Wokshop Cantina (p89)
> Cofoco (p103)
> Morgenstedet (p98)

BEST FOR SWEET TOOTHS
> Siciliansk Is (p133)
> Lagkagehuset (p98)
> Taste (p89)

BEST FOR DINING IN SOMEONE'S KITCHEN
> 1.th (p85)

V

SNAPSHOTS

GAY LIFE

Copenhagen is a popular gay getaway. Gays and lesbians are totally accepted in Danish society and there is a small but active gay scene here – predominantly, it has to be said, focused on gay men. The Landsforeningen for Bøsser and Lesbiske (Union of Gays and Lesbians; www.lbl.dk) was founded back in 1948 to promote gay rights, with great success – Denmark was the first country to legally recognise same-sex partnerships, and adoption by gay couples is also allowed.

The main gay and lesbian festival is Copenhagen Pride (www.copenhagen-pride.dk), a cultural festival held over four days in August. The event includes a Mardi Gras–style parade through the streets on the Saturday. The Copenhagen Gay & Lesbian Film Festival (www.cglff.dk) is held each year in October. The most popular gay cruising area in the city is HC Ørsteds Park. In 2009 the city hosted the second World Outgames – the gay Olympics (www.copenhagen2009.org). For more information on the scene in Copenhagen visit www.copenhagen-gay-life.dk and www.gayguide.dk.

BEST GAY VENUES
> Oscar Bar Café (www.oscarbarcafe.dk)
> Never Mind (p68)
> Jailhouse CPH (p68)
> Cosy Bar (www.myspace.com/cosybar)
> Café Intime (www.cafeintime.dk)

Off to visit the Queen at Amalienborg Slot on Dronning Margrethe II's Birthday

BACKGROUND

HISTORY

FOUNDING OF COPENHAGEN

In 1167 Bishop Absalon constructed a fortress on Slotsholmen to protect against pirates from the Baltic. In the years that followed, the harbourside village expanded and took on the name Købmandshavn (Merchants' Port). The port did much of its trade in salted herring, which was in high demand, in part due to the religious restrictions against eating meat during Catholic holy days, such as Lent.

In 1376 construction began on a new Slotsholmen fortification. King Erik of Pomerania took up residence at the castle in 1416, marking the beginning of Copenhagen's role as the capital of Denmark.

A pivotal power struggle involving the monarchy and the Catholic Church was played out during the Danish Reformation. Frederik I ascended the throne in 1523 and invited Lutheran preachers to Denmark. Their fiery messages against the corrupt power of the Catholic Church found a ready ear among the disenchanted. The country, already strained by social unrest, erupted into civil war in 1534. Eventually the Danish Lutheran church was established as the only state-sanctioned denomination.

It was during the reign of Christian IV (1588–1648) that Copenhagen was endowed with much of its splendour. Christian ascended the throne at the age of 10 and ruled for more than 50 years. Many of Copenhagen's most lavish buildings were erected during his reign. The king also extended the city significantly, developing the district of Christianshavn, which he modelled on Amsterdam. Among the many grand buildings that have survived through the centuries are Børsen (p74), Rosenborg Slot (p120) and the Rundetårn (p11).

Unfortunately, the king's foreign policies weren't nearly as brilliant. He dragged Denmark into a protracted struggle that came to be known as the Thirty Years' War. On 26 February 1658 the Treaty of Roskilde, the most lamented treaty in Denmark's history, was signed by his successor, Frederik III. The territorial losses were staggering, with Denmark's borders shrinking by a third.

In 1728 a sweeping fire razed most of Copenhagen's medieval buildings, levelling a third of the city, including the centre of government at Slotsholmen. A new and grander edifice, Christiansborg Slot, was built to replace it, and the city began to rebuild. Then in 1795 a second fire ravaged the city's remaining timber buildings, destroying the final remnants of Absalon's medieval town and the new Christiansborg Slot as well.

Copenhagen recovered from this fire only to be bombarded by the British navy in both 1801 and 1807 – resentment still lingers over that one.

By the 1830s Copenhagen had awakened to a cultural revolution in the arts, philosophy and literature, and adopted its first democratic constitution, enacted on 5 June 1849.

At the same time Copenhagen, which had previously been under royal administration, was granted the right to form a municipal council. Copenhagen's boundaries were extended into the districts of Østerbro, Vesterbro and Nørrebro to accommodate the city's growth and the new working class.

WWII

Denmark declared neutrality at the outbreak of WWII but in the early hours of 9 April 1940 the Germans landed troops at strategic points throughout Denmark. Despite the occupation, Copenhagen and the rest of Denmark emerged from WWII relatively unscathed.

Postwar Denmark saw the establishment of a comprehensive social-welfare system under the leadership and guidance of the Social Democrats.

During WWII and in the economic depression that had preceded it, many Copenhagen neighbourhoods had deteriorated into slums. In 1948 an ambitious urban renewal policy called the 'Finger Plan' was adopted and redeveloped much of the city, creating new housing projects interspaced with green areas of parks and recreational facilities that spread out like fingers from the city centre.

Denmark's monarchy continues to move with the times while providing a stable sense of tradition. In May 2004 Crown Prince Frederik and Mary Donaldson married, turning the entire city of Copenhagen into a giant party.

THE DANISH FLAG
The Danish flag, or Dannebrog, is said to be the world's oldest national flag. Legend says the first Dannebrog fell from the sky during a battle against the Estonians in 1219, which certainly saved on the design costs.

In 2006 Denmark experienced what then Prime Minister Anders Fogh Rasmussen called the most serious crisis since WWII when the Muslim world reacted with violent protests and bans on Danish goods when the Danish right-wing newspaper *Jyllands Posten* published cartoons depicting the Prophet Mohammed.

VISUAL ARTS

Copenhagen is the undisputed centre of the Danish contemporary art scene. In Christianshavn and Islands Brygge in particular, you can't throw a paintbrush without hitting an artist of some kind (though probably not the kind who uses a paintbrush). Leading the pack is Olafur Eliasson, best known for his Weather Project installation in London's Tate Modern. Funding ensures that the artist starving in a garret is a rare thing in Denmark and there are dozens of galleries and public art spaces in the city, including Charlottenborg (p81), Overgaden (p95) and Kunstforeningen (p54).

Some refer to the present day as the new 'Golden Age' of Danish art, looking to the first half of the 19th century when artists such as Christoffer Eckersberg (1783–1853) and Christian Købke (1810–48) painted scenes of everyday life with startling clarity and power. You can see paintings from this period in Statens Museum for Kunst (p120) and Den Hirschsprungske Samling (p118). The leading sculptor of the day was Bertel Thorvaldsen (1770–1844), who spent most of his working life in Rome producing work inspired by classical antiquity. When he returned to Copenhagen he established his own museum (p77). Another important art movement that evolved in the Danish capital was Cobra (formed by artists in Copenhagen, Brussels and Amsterdam), formed in 1948 by, among others, the Danish abstract artist Asger Jørn (1914–73). There are several Cobra pieces in Statens Museum (p120) and Louisiana Museum for Modern Art (p14).

DESIGN

Never consciously fashionable, but always ahead of contemporary trends, Danish designers offer a distinctive brand of simple, pared-down beauty and functionality in industrial design. Early 20th-century design pioneers such as Georg Jensen (see p59) paved the way for global design leaders such as Hans J Wegner, Arne Jacobsen and Verner Panton. Wegner's 1948 Round Chair, with its simple, smooth curving lines, is often cited as a prime example of Danish design. A decade later Arne Jacobsen produced his iconic Ant Stacker Chair, made from plywood and steel tubing. Indeed, if there is one item of furniture the Danes are famous for perfecting it is the Stacker Chair. Panton refined the genre to perhaps its ultimate incarnation in the Panton Chair, made in a variety of pop art colours from a single piece of plastic. Danish designers excelled in the field of lighting too – Poul Henningsen's designs still look futuristic today.

Danish design brought an organic sensibility to the functionalism of Bauhaus while simultaneously giving the arts and crafts movement a modernist makeover. The result has been not just great artistic acclaim but also big business. Brands like Lego, Bang & Olufsen, Bodum, Georg Jensen and Royal Copenhagen Porcelain are revered around the world. Excellent design venues include Danish Design Center (p42) and Kunstindustrimuseet (p82) in the antique stores on Bredgade and Ravnsborggade, but the best place to see Danish design is in its natural environment: in a Danish home. For the Danes, good design is not just for museums and institutions; they live with it day to day.

ENVIRONMENT

The Danes are an environmentally conscious people. They use public transport and cycle to a far greater extent than most of the rest of Europe. In 1971 Denmark was the first country to set up an Environment ministry. All but 8km of the 5000km coastline is safe and clean to swim in, the people have been avid recyclers since the 1970s (by 2008 Denmark aims to recycle 65% of its waste) and it currently produces around 20% of its power from wind turbines.

It is these turbines – 'windmills' seems too quaint a word for these giant, futuristic wind-blade towers, a row of which can be seen from planes landing at Copenhagen just east of the harbour – that have led Denmark to become globally associated with environmentally friendly initiatives. It is the world's biggest producer of wind turbines and the Danish energy sector is hoping to produce 50% of its energy this way by 2025.

On a slightly less happy note, the ammonia from pig manure produced by the huge pig-farming industry (there are 13 million pigs in Denmark, compared to 5.5 million people) is problematic and the smoking habit still lingers. About 25% of Danes over 13 smoke regularly. Over 12,000 of them die each year as a result of smoking-related illnesses. In April 2007 a rather tame new law banning smoking in public buildings came into force – but even the queen, a famous heavy smoker, now refrains from lighting up while on official duties.

GOVERNMENT AND POLITICS

In April 2009 Denmark's finance minister Lars Løkke Rasmussen (of the right-wing Venstre Party) became the country's prime minister after Anders Fogh Rasmussen ditched the top job to become secretary general of NATO. To date, the incumbent leader has faced several challenges to his popularity. His leadership of the 2009 UN Climate Conference in Copenhagen was undermined by the leaking of the draft Danish Text, a document prepared by the Danish government and which clearly advantaged developed nations over poorer members of the conference. In May 2010 Rasmussen's office announced major budget cuts to save the government 24 billion kroner, with significant reductions in unemployment insurance, child support payments and foreign aid.

Politically speaking, Denmark is a constitutional monarchy, with a single chamber parliamentary system, 179 MPs and befuddling array of political parties. Tradionally Danes prefer a political system based on consensus and compromise. When Lars Løkke Rasmussen's predecessor, Anders Fogh Rasmussen (no relative of the current prime minister, despite the surname) was elected to power in 2001, however, he lacked enough seats to command a majority. The result was a coalition in which Denmark's third-largest party, the conservative Folke Parti (People's Party), continues to wield a significant amount of power.

To many, the Folke Parti's criticism of multiculturalism in Denmark significantly influenced Anders Fogh Rasmussen's imposition of strict new immigration laws. Deemed among the toughest in Europe, the laws drew international controversy, with opponents including the Council of Europe's Human Rights Commissioner and the United Nations' High Commissioner for Refugees.

In 2006 Denmark made world headlines when a right-wing Jutland newspaper published inflammatory cartoons depicting the Prophet Mohammed. A few months later, a Copenhagen-based imam lit the touch paper by showing them to friends in Saudi Arabia. The resulting outcry saw the Dannebrog (Danish flag) burned in city streets throughout the Middle East.

FURTHER READING

Just as Danish art enjoyed a Golden Age in the first half of the 19th century, so too did its literature. It came with the emergence of its national poet, Adam Ohlenschläger, a romantic lyric poet and playwright, and

TOP FIVE COPENHAGEN READS

> *The Complete Fairy Tales* (Hans Christian Andersen) The most famous Danish book in the world. Several of the stories describe real places in the city.
> *Either/Or* (Søren Kierkegaard) The first great work of the father of existentialism.
> *Miss Smilla's Feeling for Snow* (Peter Høeg). A world-wide hit set largely in Christianshavn, later filmed with Julia Ormond and Richard Harris.
> *Silence in October* (Jens Christian Grøndahl) An engaging meditation on the dissolution of a marriage, as a man pieces together his wife's disappearance and his own inner life. Features numerous Copenhagen locations, especially around the city lakes.
> *Prince* (Ib Michael) Denmark's leading exponent of magic realism; this was his first novel translated into English.

Hans Christian Andersen (p45), who turned his hand to just about every literary form from poems to travel writing, but was of course most famous for his fairy tales. Other poets of the time included Nicolaj Frederik Severin Grundtvig – still an important literary figure in Denmark – and Bernhard Severin Ingemann.

Another important Golden Age figure was Søren Kierkegaard (p55), whose first published work was actually a criticism of one of Andersen's novels (it was not an easy read and at the time it was claimed that only two people had read it – the author and Andersen). Around 1870 a trend towards realism emerged, focusing on contemporary issues. One of the leading figures of this new movement, Henrik Pontoppidan, won a Nobel Prize for Literature in 1917 for his epic *The Realm of the Dead*. He was joined the same year by Karl Adolph Gjellerup, and in 1944 by Johannes Vilhelm Jensen.

The most famous Danish writer of the 20th century, Karen Blixen, was also nominated for the prize. She is best known for her memoir, *Out of Africa* (made into an Oscar-winning film starring Meryl Streep and Robert Redford). One of Denmark's leading contemporary novelists is the reclusive Peter Høeg, a former ballet dancer who had a global hit with *Miss Smilla's Feeling for Snow* in 1992. This was also made into a film, directed by Bille August. Several of Høeg's works have been translated into English.

In the last decade two English writers have taken Copenhagen and its more famous residents for their theme: Rose Tremain's *Music and Silence* tells of the troubled later life of King Christian IV, while Michael Frayn's play, *Copenhagen*, imagines what went on between nuclear physicists Niels Bohr and Werner Heisenberg during WWII.

DIRECTORY
TRANSPORT
ARRIVAL & DEPARTURE
AIR

The city's international airport is **Copenhagen Kastrup** (☎ 33 21 32 31; www .cph.dk), located at the southeastern tip of the island of Amager, southeast of the city centre. You can fly to Kastrup from several UK airports including Gatwick, Heathrow, Stansted, London City, Manchester, Belfast and Edinburgh. There are three terminals at Kastrup: Terminal 1 is for domestic flights, and Terminals 2 and 3 are for international flights. Be sure to check which one you are arriving at and departing from, although they are only a three-minute walk apart.

The quickest and cheapest way to get to the western side of the city centre is to take the train that leaves from beneath Terminal 3 and whisks you into Central Station in 12 minutes. A one-way ticket costs 36kr. At the Central Station you can change to the local S-tog (S-train) service, which has 13 lines serving the city centre and suburbs.

Note that the metro does not pass through Central Station, but metro line M2 runs from the eastern side of the city to Terminal 3 of the airport (the station is called Lufthavenen). A ticket, valid 90 minutes, costs 46kr.

There is a taxi rank outside Terminal 3. The ride into the city centre costs around 250kr and takes about 20 minutes.

All the major car-hire companies have offices in the airport.

Malmö airport is well outside Malmö and over an hour away by bus from central Copenhagen.

TRAIN

All train services – whether from Sweden, via the Øresund Bridge, or from Germany – stop at Central

CLIMATE CHANGE & TRAVEL

Every form of transport that relies on carbon-based fuel generates CO2, the main cause of human-induced climate change. Modern travel is dependent on aeroplanes, which might use less fuel per kilometre per person than most cars but travel much greater distances. The altitude at which aircraft emit gases (including CO2) and particles also contributes to their climate change impact. Many websites offer 'carbon calculators' that allow people to estimate the carbon emissions generated by their journey and, for those who wish to do so, to offset the impact of the greenhouse gases emitted with contributions to portfolios of climate-friendly initiatives throughout the world. Lonely Planet offsets the carbon footprint of all staff and author travel.

ROAD, SEA & RAIL

As an alternative to flying to Copenhagen you could travel here by boat or train. If you are coming from Scandinavia, for instance, you could catch the ferry from Oslo to Copenhagen (☎ 33 42 30 10; www.dfdsseaways.com), or from Helsingborg, in Sweden, to Helsingør, 40 minutes north of Copenhagen by train (HH Ferries; ☎ 49 26 01 55; www.hhferries.dk; Scandlines; ☎ 33 15 15 15; www.scandlines.dk). Ferries leave every 20 minutes during the day and half-hourly at night. Ferries to Swinoujscie in Poland leave from Nordhavn (the northern harbour) and take about 10 hours (Polferries; ☎ +46 40 97 61 80; www.polferries.se). From Germany it is just five hours by train from Hamburg to Copenhagen Central Station, via the boat-train from Puttgarden to Rødby (DSB; ☎ 70 13 14 15; www.dsb.dk). From Britain, you can sail with DFDS from Harwich to Esbjerg on Jutland, and then take the train direct to Copenhagen – there are sailings 3-4 times per week. The trip from London to Copenhagen, including trains, takes about 25 hours.

Eurolines Scandinavia runs a bus service to and from Stockholm and Gothenburg (☎ 33 88 70 00; www.eurolines.dk; Halmtorvet 5, Vesterbro). Buses leave from Ingerslevsgade near the Central Station. Tickets must be bought in advance either via the internet or at the Halmtorvet office.

Station. For all train enquiries contact **DSB** (☎ 70 13 14 15; www.dsb.dk).

GETTING AROUND

You are best off on foot within the heart of the city centre as much of it is pedestrianised and bus-free. That said, Copenhagen's exceptional, modern transport network, served by buses, the metro and S-train, is one of its trump cards. For information on public transport within the city (on S-train and bus) visit www.rejseplanen.dk, which includes an integrated route planner for bus, metro, train and S-train.

CITY BIKES

From April to November Copenhagen Council makes 2000 free bicycles available at 110 bike racks throughout the city centre. You leave a 20kr deposit in the slot, as with a supermarket trolley, and away you go – you get your money back when you return the bike to any bike rack.

One of the most convenient rental options is at **Københavns Cykler** (Map p127, D3; ☎ 33 33 86 13; www.copenhagen-bikes.dk; Reventlowsgade 11; per day 85-230kr; 8am-5.30pm Mon-Fri, 9am-1pm Sat; Central Station), in the basement of Central Station. The bicycles are in good working order and children's seats are available for hire. A deposit of 500 to 1000kr is required. The bike cost reduces per day the more days you rent.

TICKETS & TRAVEL PASSES

As you would expect, this integrated network has a ticket system based on nine geographical zones. Most of your travel will probably be within two zones. Single tickets are valid for one hour's travel (one to two zones adult/child 12 to 15 years 24/12kr; three zones 36/24kr; children under 12 years travel free if accompanied by an adult). Also available are discounted 10-ticket cards (one to two zones adult/child 150/70kr; three zones 180/90kr), which you must stamp in the yellow machines when boarding buses or on the train/metro platforms. Tickets are valid for travel on the metro, buses and S-train (even though they may look slightly different, depending on where you buy them). One ticket allows you to travel for one hour on all three types of transport.

If you buy a Copenhagen Card (p174), all travel on local public transport is inclusive.

METRO

The driverless trains of Copenhagen's **metro** (☎ 70 15 16 15; www.m.dk; ☺ customer service line 8am-4pm Mon-Fri) whoosh passengers from the western city suburb of Vanløse through the eastern side of the city centre and on to Amager. Trains run 24 hours at intervals varying from two to 20 minutes. The main stations

of interest for visitors to the city are Nørreport, Kongens Nytorv and Christianshavn. The two lines, M1 and M2, diverge at Christianshavn. The M1 line (yellow line) terminates at Copenhagen airport (the station is called Lufthavnen). Journey time from Kongens Nytorv to the airport is 14 minutes, with a ticket price of 48kr.

S-TRAIN

The local S-train runs from the suburbs through the city centre via Østerport, Nørreport, Vesterport and Central Station. Note Vesterport Station is almost within sight of Central Station. There are seven S-train lines. Services run from around 5am to 12.30am, with all-night services on Friday and Saturday nights. See www.dsb.dk.

The S-train does not run to Copenhagen Airport.

The S-train is part of the integrated ticket zone system, together with the buses and metro, so one ticket covers you on transport on any of these three forms of transport within one hour of purchase and within the zones covered by the ticket. See Tickets and Travel passes (left) for prices.

RAIL TRAVEL TO SWEDEN

Malmö is just 40 minutes by train from Copenhagen Central Station. For information on mainline rail destinations and train travel to

Sweden visit www.rejseplanen.dk or telephone DSB.

BUS

Buses run day and night in Copenhagen. The night service is less frequent and runs from 1am to 5am. Copenhagen's yellow HT buses are part of the integrated ticket zone system together with the metro and S-train, so one ticket covers you on transport on any of these three forms of transport within one hour of purchase. See Tickets and Travel passes (opposite) for prices.

Copenhagen's buses are run by Arriva. Unfortunately, the website (www.movia.dk) is only in Danish. It does have a phone enquiries line (☎ 36 13 14 15) but there's no guarantee that the person who answers will speak English. However, you can plan bus trips in and around the capital at www .rejseplanen.dk, which has an English-language option.

TAXI

Taxis can be flagged on the street and there are ranks at various points around the city centre. If the yellow Taxa sign is lit, the taxi is available for hire. The fare starts at 24kr (37kr if ordered by phone), and costs 11.5kr per km 7am to 4pm Monday to Friday, 12.5kr from 4pm to 7am Monday to Friday and all day Saturday and Sunday,

15.8kr from 11pm to 7am Friday evening to Saturday morning and public holidays. Most taxis accept major credit cards. Four of the main companies:

Codan Taxi (☎ 70 25 25 25)
Hovedstadens Taxi (☎ 38 77 77 77)
Taxa 4x35 (☎ 35 35 35 35)
Taxamotor (☎ 38 10 10 10)

BICYCLE RICKSHAW

During the summer, you can hail a **Quickshaw** (☎ 35 43 01 22; www.rickshaw .dk) or a **bicycle taxi** (☎ 27 31 38 33; www.flyingtigers-cykeltaxa.dk) for travel within the city centre. Fares vary.

HARBOUR BUSES

The **harbour water-bus service** (☎ 32 96 30 00; www.canaltours.com) runs north from Nyhavn to Nordatlantisk Brygge, the Opera House, the Little Mermaid, Langelinie (Cruise Ship Harbour), Halvandet and Amaliehaven (Royal Palace), then south to Christianshavns Torv, the Black Diamond (Det Kongelige Bibliotek), Islands Brygge, Fisketorvet, Marriott Hotel and Gammel Strand.

Buy tickets at the DFDS ticket booth at Nyhavn or on board. Single tickets (adult/child 40/30kr) are valid for one tour only, while one-day tickets (adult/child 60/40kr) allow unlimited rides. From Nyhavn, boats sail every 45 to 60 minutes from 10am to 5.30pm, mid-May to early September. See also Canal Tours (p177).

PRACTICALITIES

BUSINESS HOURS

In general, shops in Copenhagen open 9.30 or 10am until 6pm or 7pm from Monday to Friday, and until 3pm or 4pm on Saturday. Most shops are closed on Sundays apart from bakeries and florists. Some local 'kiosks', grocers and branches of Netto supermarket do remain open on Sundays, as do the shops in Central Station. In a relaxation of the Sunday opening rules, shops are allowed to open for a certain number of Sundays per year, but few take advantage of this. Office hours are typically 9am or 10am to 4pm or 5pm from Monday to Friday.

Note that the Danes tend to eat out early, starting at around 7pm or 7.30pm. Most kitchens close at 10pm and most restaurants expect you to leave by 11.30pm or midnight.

DISCOUNTS

The Copenhagen Card (adult/child 10 to 15 years per 24 hour 239/125kr; per 72 hour 469/235kr) gives you free access to around 60 museums in the city and surrounding area as well as free travel on S-train, metro and bus journeys within the nine travel zones. Note that many of the museums are free or have a free day per week so the value of this is questionable.

ELECTRICITY

Denmark, like most of Europe, runs on 220V (volts), 50Hz (cycles) AC. Check the voltage and cycle (usually 50Hz) used in your home country. Most appliances that are set up for 240V (such as those used in the UK) will handle 220V without modifications and vice versa. It's always preferable to adjust your appliance to the exact voltage if you can – a few items, such as some electric razors and radios, will do this automatically. If your appliance doesn't have a built-in transformer, don't plug a 110/125V appliance (the kind used in the USA and Canada) into a Danish outlet without using a separate transformer.

Denmark uses the 'europlug' with two round pins. Many europlugs and some sockets don't have provision for earth wiring because most local home appliances are double-insulated; when provided, earth usually consists of two contact points along the edge.

If your plugs are of a different design, you'll need an adaptor.

EMERGENCY

Copenhagen is a comparatively safe city, the main risk of crime being from drunkenness or pickpockets – and that is really only late at night and in the main tourist areas. To contact police, the ambulance service or the fire brigade, dial ☎ 112.

The nearest **Central Police Station** (Map p127, D3; ☎ 33 25 14 48) is at Halmtorvet 20, Vesterbro. There is a 24-hour pharmacy, **Steno Apotek** (Map p41, B4; ☎ 33 14 82 66; Vesterbrogade 6, Vesterbro), close to the Central Station. The nearest hospital with an accident and emergency department to the city centre is **Frederiksberg Hospital** (Map p127, B1; ☎ 38 16 35 22; www.frederiksberghospital .dk; Nordre Fasanvej 58, Frederiksberg; M Fasanvej; 29 from Rådhuspladsen).

For emergencies:
Ambulance, fire & police (☎ 112)

HOLIDAYS

Summer holidays for school children begin around 20 June and end around 10 August. Schools break for a week in mid-October, during the Christmas and New Year period, and for a week, mid-term in late February. Many Danes take their main holiday during the first three weeks of July.

Banks and most businesses are closed on public holidays, and transport schedules are commonly reduced as well.

Country-wide public holidays include:
New Year's Day (Nytårsdag) 1 January
Maundy Thursday (Skårtorsdag) The Thursday before Easter Day
Good Friday (Langfredag) The Friday before Easter Day
Easter Day (Påskedag) A Sunday in March or April
Easter Monday (2.påskedag) The day after Easter Day
Common Prayer Day (Stor Bededag) The fourth Friday after Easter
Ascension Day (Kristi Himmelfartsdag) The sixth Thursday after Easter
Whitsunday (Pinsedag) The seventh Sunday after Easter
Whitmonday (2.pinsedag) The eighth Monday after Easter
Constitution Day (Grundlovsdag) 5 June
Christmas Eve 24 December (from noon)
Christmas Day (Juledag) 25 December
Boxing Day (2.juledag) 26 December

INTERNET ACCESS

Many cafes and hotels have wireless internet access.

The most central internet cafe is **Sidewalk Express** (Map p41, B4; ☎ 80 88 27 04; www.sidewalkexpress.com; Central Station, Bernstorffsgade; per 90mins 29kr; 11am-5.30pm Mon-Thu, to 6pm Fri, 10am-3pm Sat) in the Central Station.

LANGUAGE
BASICS

Hello. (polite/ informal)	*Goddag/Hej.*
Goodbye.	*Farvel.*
Excuse me/Sorry.	*Undskyld.*
Yes.	*Ja.*
No.	*Nej.*
Thank you.	*Tak.*
You're welcome.	*Selv tak.*
Where are you from? (pol/inf)	*Hvor kommer De/du fra?*
I'm from ...	*Jeg er fra ...*

| Do you speak English? | *Taler De engelsk?* |
| I don't understand. | *Jeg forstår ikke.* |

EATING & DRINKING

That was delicious!	*Det var lækkert!*
I'm a vegetarian.	*Jeg er vegetar.*
Please bring the bill.	*Regningen, tak.*
Delicious!	*Lækkert!*

Local Specialties

Æggekage	Scrambled egg dish with bacon
Flæskesteg	Roast pork, usually with crackling, served with potatoes and cabbage
Frikadeller	Fried minced-pork meatballs, commonly served with boiled potatoes and red cabbage
Gravad laks	Cured or salted salmon marinated in dill, served with a sweet mustard sauce
Stegt flæsk	Crisp-fried pork slices, generally served with potatoes and a parsley sauce

SHOPPING

| How much is it? | *Hvor meget koster det?* |
| That's too expensive. | *Det er for dyrt.* |

EMERGENCIES

I'm sick.	*Jeg er syg.*
Help!	*Hjælp!*
Call the police.	*Ring efter politiet!*
Call an ambulance.	*Ring efter en ambulance!*

DAYS & NUMBERS

today	*i dag*
tomorrow	*i morgen*
yesterday	*i går*

0	*nul*
1	*en*
2	*to*
3	*tre*
4	*fire*
5	*fem*
6	*seks*
7	*syv*
8	*otte*
9	*ni*
10	*ti*
11	*elve*
12	*tolv*
20	*tyve*
21	*enogtyve*
100	*hundrede*
1000	*tusind*

MONEY

The Danish krone is usually written DKK in international money markets, Dkr in northern Europe and kr within Denmark.

The krone is divided into 100 øre. There are 25-øre, 50-øre, one-krone, two-kroner, five-kroner, 10-kroner and 20-kroner coins. Notes come in 50-, 100-, 200-, 500- and 1000-kroner denominations.

BANKS & ATMS

Banks can be found throughout central Copenhagen. Most are open from 10am to 4pm weekdays (to 6pm on Thursday). Most have ATMs, many of them accessible 24 hours a day and in a multitude of languages. Banks at the airport and Central Station are open longer hours and at weekends.

CHANGING MONEY

The Danske Bank branch at the airport will change currency and give advances on credit cards. If you're on an international ferry to Denmark, you'll typically be able to exchange US dollars and local currencies to Danish kroner on board. The US dollar is generally the handiest foreign currency to bring. However, Danish banks will convert a wide range of other currencies as well, including the euro, Australian dollar, British pound, Canadian dollar, Japanese yen, Swedish kroner and Swiss franc.

The following branches are convenient and reliable:

Danske Bank Airport (Arrival & Transit Halls; ☒ 6am-10pm)
Forex Central Station (☎ 33 11 22 20; Central Station; ☒ 8am-9pm)

Forex Gothersgade (☎ 33 11 27 00; Gothersgade 8; ☒ 10am-6pm Mon-Fri)
Forex Nørreport (☎ 33 32 81 00; Nørre Voldgade 90; ☒ 9am-7pm Mon-Fri, 10am-4pm Sat)

CREDIT CARDS

Credit cards such as Visa and MasterCard are generally widely accepted in Denmark, though their use often incurs a 3.5% surcharge. Many shops and supermarkets only accept the local bank card Dankort. Charge cards such as Amex and Diners Club are also accepted, but not as often.

If a card is lost or stolen, inform the issuing company as soon as possible. Here are Copenhagen numbers for cancelling your cards:

Amex (☎ 70 20 70 97)
Diners Club (☎ 36 73 73 73)
MasterCard, Access, Eurocard (☎ 80 01 60 98)
Visa (☎ 80 01 02 77)

ORGANISED TOURS

CANAL TOURS

You can't visit Copenhagen and not take a canal boat trip. Not only is it a fantastic way to see the city, but you also see a side of it land-lubbers never see. There are two companies that operate guided canal tours during the summer – **DFDS** (☎ 32 96 30 00; www.canaltours .com; embarking points Nyhavn & Gammel Strand; adult/child 60/40kr; ☒ 9.15am & up to every ¼hr until 5.30pm mid-May–mid-Jun, to 7.30pm mid-Jun–early Sep, to 5pm mid-Mar–mid-May & early Sep-Oct, 10am & every 1¼hr until 3pm Nov–mid-Mar; Ⓜ Kongens Nytorv 🚌 15, 19, 26, 1A) and **Netto Boats** (☎ 32 54 41 02; www.havnerundfart.dk; embarking points at Holmens Kirke & Nyhavn; adult/child 30/15kr; 🕙 10am-5pm 2-5 times per hr, end Mar–mid-Oct, to 7pm Jul & Aug; 🚌 6A).

Be aware that, in most boats, you are totally exposed to the elements (which can be quite elemental in Copenhagen harbour, even during the summer). DFDS also runs themed tours, including live jazz, and lunch and dinner cruises. Check their website for details. Both companies cover the same routes taking in the main sights including Nyhavn, the Little Mermaid, Holmen, Christianshavn, the harbour and the canal around Slotsholmen. DFDS also offers tours in covered, heated boats during the winter (10am and then every 75 minutes until 3pm November to mid-March); tours from the Marriott Hotel (9am from mid-March to October); and 10 daily hop-on, hop-off water buses from 10am to 5.30pm mid-May to early September (see www.canaltours .com for route information and a detailed timetable).

WALKING & CYCLING TOURS
Students from the University of Copenhagen offer **Jogging Tours** (☎ 20 29 64 19; www.joggingtours.dk;

200kr) following three tours – a Royal Tour, Nørrebro Tour and Frederiksberg Tour.

Jazz fans can explore the city's rich jazz past with a **Jazz Tour** (☎ 33 45 43 19; www.jazzguides.dk; 850kr), which includes a two- to three-course dinner with wine and entrance to two to three clubs, and is run by the Danish Jazz Union.

Copenhagen Walking Tours (☎ 40 81 12 17; www.copenhagen-walkingtours .dk) organises a range of themed tours of the city for, typically, around 100kr per person. **History Tours** (☎ 28 49 44 35; www.historytours. dk; prices vary) leads historically themed walking tours of the city centre, leaving from Højbro Plads. If you don't fancy walking, **Bike Copenhagen with Mike** (☎ 26 39 56 88; www.bikecopenhagenwithmike.dk) offers themed cycling tours of the city, departing from Turesensgade 10 (Map p127, D2), just west of Ørsteds Parken. Tours can be adapted to a theme of your choice.

Nightlife Friend (www.nightlifefriend .is) is a tour company with a differ-ence. It started in Reykjavik and has now spread to Copenhagen and Stockholm. For $US450, a local nightlife-lover will chaperon you and up to four friends around the city's hot spots for the weekend (from 10pm to 3am Friday & Satur-day), with VIP entrance to clubs.

Ghost Tours (adult/child 100/70kr) operates a 1½-hour walking tour of haunted sites in Copenhagen, leaving from Nyhavn at 8pm by advance booking only. English-language tours usually run only in the summer months.

TELEPHONE

The international dialling code for Denmark is +45. Public phones are either coin operated or require a *telekort* phonecard, which you can buy at kiosks and post offices.

TIPPING

Service is included in restaurant bills, and Copenhageners are fairly mean tippers, but you might like to leave 10% if you feel the service has been good.

TOURIST INFORMATION

The **Copenhagen Visitor Centre** (Map p41, B3; ☎ 70 22 24 42; www.visitcopenhagen .com; Vesterbrogade 4A; ☻ 9am-4pm Mon-Fri, to 2pm Sat Jan-Apr & end Sep-Dec, 9am-6pm Mon-Sat, 10am-2pm Sun May & Jun, 9am-8pm Mon-Sat, 10am-6pm Sun Jul & Aug, 9am-6pm Mon-Sat early-end Sep; ⓡ S-train Central Station, Vesterport; ⓑ 1A, 2A, 5A, 6A), just across from the Tivoli main entrance, offers information on Copenhagen and Denmark, as well as a last-minute hotel book-ing service with rooms often at half-price.

TRAVELLERS WITH DISABILITIES

Copenhagen tries to be a disability -friendly city, but facilities do vary greatly and many buildings in the city centre are hindered by the fact that they either have cellar- or raised first-floor entrances, which are usually quite narrow and don't allow for ramps. Main major sights and museums are usually well equipped but the older hotels and shops in the city centre are often not accessible. The **Dansk Handicap Forbund** (☎ 39 29 35 55; danskhandicap forbund.dk; Kollektivhuset, Hans Knudsens Plads 1A) manages a website (www .tbasen.dk) that lists hotels, restaurants, museums, churches and entertainment venues that are accessible to travellers with disabilities in the greater Copen-hagen area. The website is in Dan-ish, but queries can be emailed directly to the organisation. The **Danish Accessibility Association** (☎ 35 24 80 90; www.godadgang.dk; Vodroffsvej 32) also provides information about disability-friendly venues and services.

>INDEX

See also separate subindexes for See (p189), Shop (p190), Eat (p191), Drink (p192) and Play (p192).

000 map pages

SEE

SHOP

Art & Design
Designer Zoo 130

000 map pages